THE
COMING
REVIVAL

DEREK PRINCE

THE
COMING
REVIVAL

SHAPING HISTORY FOR A NEW HEAVENLY REALITY

WHITAKER
HOUSE

Publisher's Note: This book was compiled from the extensive archive of Derek Prince's unpublished materials and approved by the Derek Prince Ministries editorial team.

THE COMING REVIVAL:
Shaping History for a New Heavenly Reality

Derek Prince Ministries
P.O. Box 19501
Charlotte, North Carolina 28219-9501
www.derekprince.org

ISBN: 978-1-64123-211-1
eBook 978-1-64123-212-8
Printed in the United States of America
© 2019 by Derek Prince Ministries–International

Whitaker House
1030 Hunt Valley Circle
New Kensington, PA 15068
www.whitakerhouse.com

Library of Congress Cataloging-in-Publication Data (Pending)

1 2 3 4 5 6 7 8 9 10 11 ⨃ 26 25 24 23 22 21 20 19

CONTENTS

FOREWORD

While Derek Prince was living in London in 1953, the Lord spoke these words to him: "There shall be a great revival in the United States and Great Britain."

Derek testified that this was the only time he ever heard the audible voice of God, even though he sensed His direction and promptings many other times throughout his life. And the promise God spoke to him then came with absolute authenticity and authority.

Do you believe the Lord wants to bring revival? On the basis of God's promise, Derek believed it. What's more, he felt the word spoken to him in 1953 was yet to be fulfilled.

If it is true that the revival we seek is still around the corner, then the years to come will hold great excitement for us. The renewal God wants to bring to the United States and Great Britain—indeed, to the whole world—lies just ahead for all of us.

Is it possible we have a pivotal role to play in this coming revival? If so, how should we prepare ourselves to be used by the Lord in the revolutionary times to come? You will find thoroughly biblical and practical answers to these questions in this riveting book, *The Coming Revival*, containing the teachings of Derek Prince.

Derek knew there would be many contributing factors to the worldwide revival God intends to bring. However, in these teachings, he chose to focus on just seven elements essential to the process. These elements fall into two categories: positive aspects we must incorporate into our Christian experience and negative aspects we need to remove from our lives and testimony.

Here are the seven pivotal factors Derek highlighted which comprise the seven parts of this book:

1. "Loving Others": recognizing the foundation of true revival

2. "Loving God": giving ourselves fully and obediently in preparation for revival

3. "Humbling Ourselves": surrendering pride, a major obstacle to revival

4. "Eliminating Legalism": removing a self-righteous and self-sufficient mind-set, a second obstacle to revival

5. "Unmasking Witchcraft": eradicating witchcraft (control and manipulation in all its forms), a third obstacle to revival

6. "Getting Desperate": becoming hungry for revival

7. "Purifying Ourselves": coming into total commitment to God, leading to revival

What might happen within the church and in the world if we would apply just these seven principles? Imagine the impact it would make if we would simply take the positive steps of loving one another, obeying the Lord, calling out to God in sincerity, and purifying ourselves, as well as eliminating the negative forces of pride, legalism, and manipulation from our midst!

Are you ready to prepare your heart for the revival just ahead? Will you start the process by focusing on the steps Derek has suggested?

"There shall be a great revival in the United States and Great Britain." Let it begin with us—as we respond in faith, taking the seven initial steps outlined in this book.

—The International Publishing Team of Derek Prince Ministries

PART ONE:

LOVING OTHERS

1

THE FOUNDATION OF REVIVAL

It may surprise you that a book on revival would begin with a discussion of love. But loving others is actually the foundation and beginning point for true revival. I believe that if we are going to see the revival our hearts long for, we must address seven essential issues, the first two of which involve a deeper commitment to and development of love: (1) loving others, (2) loving God, (3) humbling ourselves, (4) eliminating legalism, (5) unmasking witchcraft, (6) getting desperate, and (7) purifying ourselves. In this chapter, we will begin an in-depth look at the first of those seven issues.

LOVE IS CENTRAL

Love—that small but powerful word—takes center stage in the pages that follow. For the church to respond to a dying world in desperate need of revival, something life-changing must happen to us deep in our hearts. We need a fresh encounter with genuine love—God's own love. This irresistible love is "ground zero," the very starting point for revival. Only when we receive the love of God (see Romans 5:5) can we love other people.

We will begin our exploration of the vital quality of love with a passage in 1 John 4. Various forms of the word *love* appear twenty-eight times throughout this chapter. For our purposes, we will read only six verses. However, I recommend that you review the full chapter on your own so you can see for yourself how often this term appears. It is quite remarkable.

Clearly, love is central to the nature of God—and loving others is an essential principle for preparing our hearts for revival.

> *Beloved, let us love one another, for love is of God; and everyone who loves is born of God and knows God. He who does not love does not know God, for God is love. In this the love of God was manifested toward us, that God has sent His only begotten Son into the world, that we might live through Him. In this is love, not that we loved God, but that He loved us and sent His Son to be the propitiation for our sins. Beloved, if God so loved us, we also ought to love one another.... And we have known and believed the love that God has for us. God is love, and he who abides in love abides in God, and God in him.*
>
> (1 John 4:7–11, 16)

LOVE CHANGES HEARTS

When I read passages like this about the depth of God's love for us, I tend to get emotional. Years ago, I would not have had such a response. God had to do a deep work in my heart, because I was brought up not to show emotion. Although I came from a good family, we never discussed or demonstrated love for one another. I won't go into all my background, but I am from a military family, and I was educated in boarding schools and universities in England from the age of nine until the age of twenty-five. If ever anyone was trained in "The School of the Stiff Upper Lip," it was I. Emotion had very little place in my life.

God filled this pronounced lack of receiving and demonstrating love in my life on the last Thursday night of July 1941. In a British army barracks room in the middle of the night, I had a dramatic personal encounter with Jesus Christ that totally and permanently changed my life. I am certainly not perfect, but I am markedly different from what I was before I met Jesus—especially in my ability to receive and express God's love.

"A GREAT REVIVAL"

From that point in my life, let us fast forward twelve years to 1953. At that time, I was pastoring a small assembly of believers in the Bayswater area of London. One night, around two in the morning, the Lord woke me up and spoke to me. That was the only time in my life I actually heard God speak to me audibly, and I have never forgotten one word of what He said.

I will quote some of His message here. There was no introduction or explanation about what He spoke. God simply said this: "There shall be a great revival in the United States and Great Britain." Then He gave me some personal instruction for my ministry, and He ended with these words: "But the condition is obedience in small things and in great things; for the small things are as great as the great things."

I have never doubted that God spoke those words to me, even though decades have passed. For me, this passage of time is particularly important in light of the statement Caleb made before going into the promised land. He declared, in effect, "Forty-five years have passed, but I intend to go into the inheritance." (See Joshua 14:6–15.) Entering into God's inheritance is my intention, too.

You might be saying to yourself, "That's all well and good, but that was years ago, and the world is still falling apart. Where is the revival God promised?"

I will tell you what I believe: God is going to send a great revival—but He is not going to send it to the nations. He is going to send revival to the church *in* the nations. This is a very important distinction, because it is revival in the church that will impact the nations of the world.

MEETING GOD'S CONDITIONS

Like me, you have probably heard various prophecies about revival. I have heard people prophesy, "There is going to be revival here," or "There will be a revival there." I have believed some of these prophecies, yet I have questioned others. Maybe you feel the same way about what you have heard.

The problem is that as exciting as these prophecies may sound, they can be self-defeating. Why? Because just to say, "There is going to be a revival," tends to let people off the hook of their personal responsibility in relation to revival. These kinds of prophecies leave people thinking, "Well, thank goodness *I* don't have to do much of anything to make revival happen, since it's going to happen anyway!"

But this is a faulty perspective. I believe in God's promise that there will be revival. But it will happen *only when God's people meet His conditions.* No prayer or prophecy can bypass God's conditions. Revival will not take place automatically. It will come as God's people fulfill His requirements. When the Lord spoke that word to me many years ago, He concluded by saying, "But the condition is obedience in small things and in great things; for the small things are as great as the great things."

If we take an honest look at our troubled world, it is evident that we can no longer just sit back and wait for God to send revival. That is clearly not what God is asking us to do! Even so, as the world languishes, the church seems to remain in a state of confusion about what steps it needs to take. It is fairly obvious the church has not yet met the conditions God spoke of that night in 1953. Even though we have earnestly prayed, fasted, and prophesied, something is still missing.

I believe the Holy Spirit has revealed the essential issues we must face if we truly expect revival to come—the seven elements described in the preface to this book and at the beginning of this chapter. It is my hope that *The Coming Revival* will renew a hope and an expectation in your heart for revival. Our heavenly Father longs to send revival to our troubled world. He is ready and waiting—if you and I will simply meet the conditions.

2

THE REAL REQUIREMENT

In chapter 1, we noted that our starting point for revival is God's love. Any revival—whether in the life of a person, a church, or a nation—begins with a change of heart. And only the supernatural power of God's love can spark that change. We also saw that although God has promised to send revival, as is the case with all biblical promises, there are conditions He first waits for us to meet.

UNDERSTANDING RIGHTEOUSNESS

However, before we go deeper into our exploration of the first condition, we must deal with a misconception in the church about the meaning of "righteousness," or right standing with God. This misconception has a direct connection with our first principle of loving one another. Why? Because there is a strong tie-in between righteousness and love.

Through the years, I have found that most Christians don't really understand the concept of righteousness. They assume that to be righteous means to follow a set of rules. But it is actually much different from that. The key verses for this part of our study come from the book of Romans, whose core theme is righteousness. Actually, in these verses, you might be surprised to learn what God does *not* require of us:

For what the law could not do in that it was weak through the flesh,
God did by sending His own Son in the likeness of sinful flesh, on ac-
count of sin: He condemned sin in the flesh, that the righteous require-
ment of the law might be fulfilled in us who do not walk according to
the flesh but according to the Spirit.   (Romans 8:3–4)

As I understand this passage, Paul is saying that God has never expected us to achieve righteousness by keeping the law of Moses. The law of
Moses was perfect. It was God-given. Thus, the fault is not in the law—the
fault is in us. But because God knew we could not achieve righteousness by
keeping the law, He provided an alternative way through the substitution-
ary sacrifice of His Son Jesus on the cross.

I believe that Jesus Himself was the only Jewish person who ever perfectly kept the law of Moses. Then, He gave His life as an atonement for
the sins of all those who had broken the law and also the sins of those who
had never been under the law.

Therefore, we are not required to achieve righteousness by obeying the
law of Moses. That's a relief, isn't it? The law of Moses was extremely tough.
Even if it were possible for anyone to obey it to the letter, no one ever has.
(See Romans 3:11–12.)

JOB'S QUESTION

If, then, we are not required to keep the law of Moses, what *are* we required to do? How can we achieve righteousness with God? Four thousand
years ago, out of his perplexity and misery, a man named Job asked the
same question:

How can a man be righteous before God?   (Job 9:2)

Job's friends—if you can call them friends—ridiculed the idea that
anybody could ever be righteous before God. But many hundreds of years
later, God gave His answer to this question: "*The righteousness of God is revealed from faith to faith; as it is written, 'The just shall live by faith'*" (Romans
1:17).

Through the writings of the apostle Paul, God tells us we are not required to observe the law because righteousness comes by faith. However, as we just read in Romans 8:4, Paul also says, *"...that the righteous requirement of the law might be fulfilled in us who do not walk according to the flesh but **according to the Spirit**."* So, we are not required to observe the law, but we *are* required to fulfill *"the righteous requirement of the law."*

To better understand this truth—and to see its direct connection with the principle of loving one another—let's look at the original Greek words translated *"righteous"* and *"righteousness."* Paul uses the term *dikaiosyne* for *"righteousness"* and *dikaioma* for *"righteous." Dikaiosyne* is somewhat of a general concept, while *dikaioma* is a specific outworking of it. The word *dikaioma* is used in Revelation 19:8 where it says, *"The fine linen of the saints is the righteous acts of the saints."*

Therefore, the word Paul uses in Romans 8:4, *dikaioma*, means righteousness in action, righteousness worked out, righteousness made practical. It is the practical outworking of the law that we are required to observe, rather than the letter of the commandment. Now that we understand this distinction, let's read our key Scripture passage one more time:

> *For what the law could not do in that it was weak through the flesh, God did by sending His own Son in the likeness of sinful flesh, on account of sin: He condemned sin in the flesh, that the righteous requirement of the law might be fulfilled in us who do not walk according to the flesh but according to the Spirit.* (Romans 8:3–4)

THE FIRST STEP TO REVIVAL

We understand we are not required to keep the law of Moses—but we *are* required to keep the righteous requirement of the law. This leads us to a question whose answer is vital for every Christian: What is the righteous requirement of the law? (What exactly are we required to fulfill?)

The answer to this question, as you may have guessed, is the theme of both parts one and two of this book. It is the primary issue for us to grasp, and the first step toward revival: *love*. Love is the righteous requirement of the law. Love is what we are expected to observe. Let us now explore more of what the Scriptures have to say about this wonderful truth!

3

THE LAW OF LOVE

What we have just learned about the righteous requirement of the law should have shattered any preconceived legalistic notions we might have had about the meaning of righteousness. Righteousness does not mean obeying a set of rules. It does not mean following "the law." It is an outworking of *love*.

We cannot underestimate the impact that Jesus's teaching about the law of love versus the law of Moses had upon His followers. It changed everything for them—their religion, their culture, their very world. Their transformed outlook and lifestyle constituted the original "revival," and this is exactly what we desperately need today.

TWO GREAT COMMANDMENTS

To illustrate the revolutionary effects of this distinction, let's look at a conversation in the book of Matthew between Jesus and a teacher of the law of Moses. Most of the religious leaders of the day who engaged Jesus in discussions were not looking for truth. Rather, they were seeking to "trap" Jesus in order to discredit Him.

Then one of them, a lawyer [or a teacher of the law], asked Him a question, testing Him, and saying, "Teacher, which is the great commandment in the law?" Jesus said to him, "You shall love the LORD

21

your God with all your heart, with all your soul, and with all your mind." This is the first and great commandment. And the second is like it: "You shall love your neighbor as yourself." (Matthew 22:35–39)

Notice that Jesus did not hedge about His answer. Neither did He compromise on it. He was absolutely clear. The two great commandments are to love the Lord your God and to love your neighbor as yourself.

ALREADY IN PLACE

In His conversation with the teacher of the law, Jesus went on to say,

On these two commandments hang all the Law and the Prophets.
(Matthew 22:40)

"The Law and the Prophets" referenced by Jesus represent what we call the Old Testament. Thus, what Jesus said to this teacher of this law, who asked his question only in order to test Jesus, was revolutionary. Jesus summarized the entire spirit of the Old Testament—the Law and the Prophets, as well as the Writings—in two single commandments.

Let me give a simple illustration of this summary. Suppose I were speaking before a large audience, and I decided to take off my jacket and hang it on a hook on the wall behind me. In considering this illustration, one simple fact stands out: the hook would already need to be in place on the wall before I could hang my jacket on it. So it is with what Jesus said to the teacher of the law. All of the Law and the Prophets could hang on these two commandments because they were already in place. Therefore, the *primary commandments*, which existed *before* the Law and the Prophets, are the two great commandments Jesus cited: love God and love our neighbor as ourselves.

THE DEBT OF LOVE

Next, let us look at a passage about love and law from Romans 13. Paul starts this passage with a rather strong statement: *"Owe no one anything"* (verse 8). In other words, don't be in debt. That is always good advice, but monetary debt isn't what Paul is really speaking about here. Let's read the passage in its entirety:

> *Owe no one anything except to love one another, for he who loves an-other has fulfilled the law. For the commandments, "You shall not commit adultery," "You shall not murder," "You shall not steal," "You shall not bear false witness," "You shall not covet," and if there is any other commandment, are all summed up in this saying, namely, "You shall love your neighbor as yourself." Love does no harm to a neighbor; there-fore love is the fulfillment of the law.*   (Romans 13:8–10)

There you have it: love is the righteous requirement of the law, "*for he who loves another has fulfilled the law.*"

We could review many other Scriptures with the same theme, but let's look at Galatians 5:14, where Paul says very clearly,

> *For all the law is fulfilled in one word, even in this: "You shall love your neighbor as yourself."*

Notice that the whole law is fulfilled in essentially one word. What is that word? "*Love.*"

A NEW COMMANDMENT

When Jesus was in the upper room with His disciples on the night of the Last Supper, He spoke to them about the establishment of the new covenant. Up to that moment, the old covenant—the Law, the Prophets, and the Writings—had been the bedrock and essence of their faith—everything they knew about God. Yet that whole mind-set changed with these words of Jesus in John 13:34:

> *A new commandment I give to you....*

The disciples knew Moses had given them the Ten Commandments, plus a whole set of regulations. Even today, Judaism has 613 commandments based on the Pentateuch, or the first five books of the Old Testament. Yet Jesus was saying, in effect, "I'll give you only one commandment. That's all. If you will fulfill this, that's all I ask." What is this one commandment? To love one another the way Jesus has loved us:

> *A new commandment I give to you, that you love one another; as I have loved you, that you also love one another.* (John 13:34)

Jesus went on to say,

> *By this all will know that you are My disciples, if you have love for one another.* (verse 35)

THE EVANGELISM OF LOVE

During the years of my ministry, I have had the privilege to work with various evangelistic organizations, many of which had a powerful vision for evangelism that I shared. I have evangelized in many ways, in many places, and to many people. But I recognized this fact: no evangelist or program for evangelism can ever reach the whole human race. There is only one force that can do that:

> *By this all will know that you are My disciples, if you have love for one another.*

It is the love of Christians for one another that will reach the entire world with the gospel of Jesus Christ.

THE GOAL IS LOVE

One of my favorite Scriptures is 1 Timothy 1:5–6:

> *Now the purpose of the commandment* [Paul's instruction for the church at Ephesus through Timothy] *is love from a pure heart, from a good conscience, and from sincere faith, from which some, having strayed, have turned aside to idle talk.*

"*The purpose of the commandment is love….*" Paul gives three requirements for having this kind of all-encompassing love: "*a pure heart,*" "*a good* conscience," and "sincere faith." I like the New American Standard Bible rendering of the beginning of 1 Timothy 1:5:

The goal of our instruction is love.

When I recently reread this verse, it caused me to pause and think. Although I have been a preacher for at least fifty years, I had to ask myself, "What has been the goal of my instruction? What have I aimed to produce in the people who listen to my teaching?" Considering Paul's admonition that the aim or goal of biblical instruction should be to produce love in people, I had to admit that I had often failed.

If you are in a leadership position in the church, or active in ministry in some other way—perhaps as a preacher, a Bible teacher, or a Sunday school teacher—I want to ask you the same questions: "What is the goal of your instruction? What are you are aiming to produce in the people who listen to your teaching?"

If you are not aiming to produce love, you are missing the mark. Paul says that anything other than love is "idle talk" (1 Timothy 1:6), or, as the New American Standard Bible translates it, "fruitless discussion." That is a very sobering thought. I suggest to you that much of contemporary Christian activity is misdirected. Why? Because it is *not* aimed at producing the one quality that has to be our objective.

EMPTY WORDS AND WASTED TIME

We know that the righteous requirement of the law is summed up as *love*. Yet, if you were to ask the non-Christians in this country, "What do you think is the attitude of Christians to one another?" very few people would answer, "Love." The unsaved, in many ways, are more observant than the saved. We get so used to the religious culture we call Christianity that we assume we are obeying God correctly. We say, "This is the way we've always done it. Why should we do it any differently?"

But I want us to closely consider the question at hand. How much time is wasted in churches because we are not producing the one trait that is required of us? First and foremost, I ask this question of myself as a teacher of the Word of God. If I am not producing love in the people who follow my ministry, listen to my radio messages, or read my books, it is all *"idle talk"* or *"fruitless discussion"*—empty words and wasted time. This is a shocking consideration.

The only answer for any of us is to seek to have in ourselves and to produce in others *"love from a pure heart, from a good conscience, and from sincere faith"* (1 Timothy 1:5).

4

FERVENT LOVE

After reading the previous chapter about the need for greater love to be produced in and practiced among Christians, you may be feeling a sense of conviction and contrition. That is a healthy response for all believers. It enables us to move toward fulfilling God's righteous requirement. Therefore, let's further explore this theme of love.

In 1 Peter 1, the apostle gives us the primary evidence of being "born again." The term *born again* might have become a cliché to many people, but if we claim to be truly born again, or born anew by the Spirit (see John 3:3–8)—we need to know what this really means.

PASSPORT TO HEAVEN?

Although I grew up in England, I have lived much of my adult life in the United States, and I have become an American citizen. Apparently, tens of millions of Americans consider themselves to be "born again" Christians.[1] My response to such claims is this: where are all these Christians and what are they doing? Because the country is going downhill with incredible rapidity!

I think the term "born again" is often used as an identifier by people who want to consider themselves spiritual but don't really want to change

---

1. The population of America today is approximately 325 million, and, according to a 2016 Barna Group report, 35 percent identify themselves as "born again."

their lifestyle. They don't want to undergo any radical transformation in their outlook or behavior. Rather, they simply want to think of themselves as nice people who are headed for heaven.

A lot of teaching in the church about the new birth absolutely misses the mark and thus deceives people. I am afraid there are many well-meaning people who think they will get to heaven, but who will be disappointed. They consider the term "born again" to be a sort of heavenly passport.

TOTAL TRANSFORMATION

In contrast to these misconceptions, here is what Peter says about the new birth:

> *Since you have purified your souls in obeying the truth through the Spirit in sincere love of the brethren, love one another fervently with a pure heart, having been born again, not of corruptible seed but incorruptible, through the word of God which lives and abides forever.*
>
> (1 Peter 1:22–23)

In one word, what is the primary evidence that we have truly been born again? "*Love.*"

If we have experienced the new birth, we will love our fellow believers. Peter indicates we wouldn't be able to love the way we love if we hadn't been born again. However, even this is not enough. He says we must continue to purify our hearts until we "*love one another fervently.*"

This shows us that being saved is more than simply a change of label from "sinner" to "born again." Salvation does not just mean answering an altar call in a church service or going through a kind of religious ritual. Instead, being saved is a total life transformation that takes you from darkness to light and makes you no longer a slave of Satan but instead a child of God.

If there is one truth that needs to be emphasized today in countries with a long Christian heritage, it is that salvation isn't what a lot of people call it. If you are mildly religious, you might be a little better off than some of your neighbors. But the truth is, your relationship with God may be very shaky. It is up to you to make certain of your salvation by trusting in Christ as your Savior and then, by God's Spirit, producing real evidence of transformation in your life.

DO YOU KNOW?

What is the primary evidence that a person really knows God? We find additional confirmation of that answer in the fourth chapter of 1 John, in the passage that started our entire study:

Beloved, let us love one another, for love is of God; and everyone who loves is born of God and knows God.   (1 John 4:7)

If you plumb the depths of that statement, you will see that it is remarkable. Just like the passage from 1 Peter, it tells us there is a kind of love a person cannot have unless he has been truly born again. Only those who have been *"born of God"* can have this kind of love. If we merely have the kind of everyday, human love that is common to people around the world, that isn't evidence we have been born again. In the next verse, John goes on to say,

He who does not love does not know God, for God is love.
                                                        (1 John 4:8)

What is the evidence that we truly know God? We have His love.

I have known a number of people from different backgrounds, denominations, and nationalities who consider themselves Christians, although it's difficult to see the evidence in their lives. I would say of many of these individuals that if they are saved, then they were "saved by a stranger." Let me give you an example to explain what I mean.

Suppose you are drowning in a river, fighting for your life, and you are sinking for the third time. Somebody plunges into the water from the riverbank, pulls you out, puts you dripping wet into the seat of his beautifully upholstered car, drives you to his home, dries you off, gives you a set of clean, warm clothes to wear, and takes care of all your needs. Then, to top it all off, this individual says, "From now on, let's be friends. You know where I live, and here is my phone number. You can phone me any time you like. Please come and see me!"

Now suppose that you never call or go back to visit the one who saved you from drowning, taking for granted everything he did for you. I would say you were "saved by a stranger." Your life was spared, but you never really came to know the person who saved you. It is a similar case for the people I mentioned above. They don't really know the Person who has saved them from sin and death.

"He who does not love does not know God." You may know a lot of Scripture. You may know a lot of theology. You may be a member of a church. But if you do not love, you do not know God—and you are much the poorer for it. Because if there is one Person who is really worthwhile getting to know, it is God!

5

FAITH WORKS THROUGH LOVE

In our endeavor to understand and embrace the kind of love that will bring revival to the world, we need to take a moment to consider the connection between faith and works. Understandably, at the mention of the word *works*, many Christians get a little nervous, because it sounds "legalistic." We know that the Bible says we are saved by faith and not by works. (See, for example, Romans 4:2–4; Ephesians 2:8.) Even so, works need to be considered in their full biblical context.

FAITH WITHOUT WORKS

Before I was saved, I was a professional philosopher and my subject was logic. I would like to say, just by way of personal testimony, that the most logical book I have ever read is the Bible. And I believe the most logical book in the Bible is Paul's epistle to the Romans. The logic found in that book is absolutely flawless. There are no inconsistencies. However, for this part of our study, I want us to look at James 2:26, which is also a completely logical statement:

For as the body without the spirit is dead, so faith without works is dead also.

Here is what James is saying in this verse (and in this whole chapter): you can *say* you have faith, but if it doesn't express itself in what you *do*, it's a dead faith. For example, you can say to somebody in need, *"'Be warmed and filled.'* Have a nice day!" (See James 2:16.) But if you don't sacrifice your time and resources and provide that person with the food and clothing they need, your words are just that—words. Empty words.

Thus, James tells us that merely professing faith is not enough. He doesn't say that to profess faith is wrong—he says it is insufficient. Your faith has to be expressed by the tangible actions you take. In the Bible, the actions we take are referred to as *"works."*

A DOCTRINE OF LOVE

What is the biblical way to express our faith through works? We find it in one of my favorite epistles, the book of Galatians. First, let me say this: if you have never been shocked by what you have read in the Bible, you have never really read the Bible, because it is a shocking book! (It's probably the most shocking for religious people.) As Mark Twain once famously (and colloquially) said, "It ain't those parts of the Bible that I can't understand that bother me; it's the parts that I do understand."

Once we understand what the Bible says about faith and works, we need to respond accordingly. Galatians 5:6 tells us this:

> *For in Christ Jesus neither circumcision nor uncircumcision avails any-thing, but faith working through love.*

How does faith work? *"Through love."*

Let's be honest. If we have faith that doesn't work through love, what kind of faith do we have? Clearly, we have a dead faith. Here is the logical sequence of thought:

1. Faith without works is dead.
2. Faith works through love.
3. Therefore, faith without love is dead.

The revelations in these statements are far more significant for our lives than we may realize. They tell us the bold truth. We might have the most meticulously accurate, doctrinal faith. We might have dotted every "i" and crossed every "t" theologically. And yet our faith might be totally dead if it isn't expressed in love.

THE GOAL OF LOVE

According to my personal observation, here is the problem, which we discussed at the end of chapter 3: the majority of church activity in the United States today does not make producing love its goal. It appears to be focused on establishing certain doctrinal truths, commenting on a current political controversy, or promoting cultural ideologies. But overall, the church does not seem aimed at love. As I have said many times, if you aim at nothing, you will surely hit it.

I don't want to seem overly critical of the church. I was christened and confirmed as an Anglican in Britain—but I was a rebel against the Anglican Church for many years. I made a lot of unkind statements about it, stemming from negative experiences growing up. They weren't untrue statements, but they were unkind. Now that I have made this confession, you might be surprised to learn that later in my life, my wife Ruth and I attended an Anglican church every week in Jerusalem, and we loved it. I think God would not let me finish my life's career without reconciling with the Anglican Church.

Today, all my complaints are laid down, as are all my criticisms. I no longer bother to make them. It is so easy to criticize the church. It doesn't require any cleverness to do that. But to *change* a church—that is a task. And that is the task before us now: to bring the goal of love to the church.

"MAKE LOVE YOUR AIM"

At this point, I would like to reach out to all Christians like myself who are Pentecostals and charismatics, who speak in tongues and believe in spiritual gifts. For a long time, I didn't know there was a way to be a Christian without speaking in tongues. That is because when I was saved, I spoke in tongues almost immediately. It took me a long while to discover there was any other kind of Christian. So, believe me, if there is anybody who believes in speaking in tongues and spiritual gifts, it is I.

Having said that, however, I would like to point out what Paul says in the opening passage of 1 Corinthians 13:

Though I speak with the tongues of men and of angels.... (verse 1)

I want to pause here to say that this is a startling comment! Do you speak in tongues? If so, has it ever occurred to you that you might be speaking in an angelic language rather than a human one? When I received Christ, I was serving with the British army. During my service in North Africa in World War Two, I had no Christian fellowship. I had to rely solely on fellowship with the Lord, and I would often pray in tongues. After a while, I observed that I used one tongue that had no "s" sounds in it, and I have often wondered whether that was an angelic language. I don't know whether it was or not, but it is at least possible, according to Scripture, to speak not merely in the tongues of men but also of angels.

Let's return to 1 Corinthians 13:1:

Though I speak with the tongues of men and of angels but have not love, I have become sounding brass or a clanging cymbal.

Without love, we are just empty noise. Someone asked me if it is possible to misuse the gifts of the Holy Spirit. The answer is definitely yes. Any use of the gifts without love is a misuse.

And though I have the gift of prophecy, and understand all mysteries and all knowledge [the spiritual gift of a word of wisdom or a word of knowledge], *and though I have all faith* [another spiritual gift], *so that I could remove mountains, but have not love, I am nothing.*
(1 Corinthians 13:2)

It is easy for us to think of other people to whom the above verse might apply. But why don't we ask ourselves if it applies to us? The apostle goes on to say,

And though I bestow all my goods to feed the poor, and though I give
my body to be burned, but have not love, it profits me nothing.
                                                      (1 Corinthians 13:3)

There are some ministers who have helped other people by the use of
their spiritual gifts—but it has not profited them. The same can be true for
anyone. Without the presence of love, it is possible for us to edify others
and yet not be spiritually benefited ourselves.

Moving on to the first verse of the next chapter, we read,

Pursue love, and desire spiritual gifts.   (1 Corinthians 14:1)

Paul is not against spiritual gifts, but he says we need to get our priorities right. Priority number one is not spiritual gifts—it is love. The *Revised
Standard Version* translates the first part of this verse as, *"Make love your
aim...."* I think that's a good translation.

Will you make love your aim? If you will make love your aim, you will
become a different person than you are now.

HOW LOVE COMES

If we want to make love our aim, we must first be able to receive God's
love. The Lord primarily imparts His love to us in two ways. The first way
is by His Holy Spirit:

The love of God has been poured out in our hearts by the Holy Spirit
who was given to us.   (Romans 5:5)

I don't think there is any limit on God's side of this equation—He
just pours out His love. The limit is on our side. How much do we want to
receive?

I have sometimes experienced the love of God being poured out in my
heart by the Holy Spirit in a tangible way. Allow me to share one brief
example with you. I mentioned above that I served with the British army
in North Africa. A few years into my service, I ended up in a very remote,
barren, inhospitable corner of what is now the Sudan. Before I was sent

to my specific assignment, which was a small military hospital in the Red Sea Hills, I was detained for a few weeks in what the British army calls a "reception station."

For the first time in three years of army life, I didn't have to sleep in my underwear. This reception station was equipped with actual nightclothes and everything else that could make you comfortable—including three real beds. Since I had no patients to tend to, I thought, "Why not enjoy some nightclothes and a bed?" So I did.

One night, I began to pray for the people of the Sudan, and the particular tribe upon whom I focused my prayers was called the Hadendoa. The people were aggressive and warlike, and they had known no religion but Islam all their lives. The men had a habit of covering their hair with mutton fat so that it stood about eight inches above their heads. To me, there was nothing outwardly attractive or appealing about this tribe.

But that night, as I began to pray, God poured out His love into my heart for them. I couldn't even lie on the bed. I had to get up and pace, praying earnestly for these people whom I did not know and whom I had no natural reason whatsoever for loving.

As I was interceding in the darkness of my room, I discovered that my white nightclothes had begun to gleam. They were supernaturally illuminated. That phenomena indicated to me that somehow, just for a few moments, I had become identified with Jesus, the Great Intercessor. Sometime later, I had the privilege of leading to the Lord the first member of the Hadendoa tribe who ever confessed Jesus Christ as Savior.

I share this experience because it provided for me, in some measure, an understanding of what it means to have *"the love of God...poured out in our hearts by the Holy Spirit."* Please understand that after this event, I was still a very imperfect, immature Christian. I continued to be irritable, selfish, self-centered, insensitive, and easily angered on occasion—even after that beautiful experience of God's outpoured love.

I am not belittling the experience, but I want to point out that it takes more than a spiritual experience to change your character. God has another means to do it, which is the second way God imparts His love to us: by His Word.

Concerning the relationship between God's Word and His love, 1 John 2:5 tells us this:

> *But whoever keeps His [God's] word, truly the love of God is perfected in him. By this we know that we are in Him.*

A POWERFUL COMBINATION

Ever since creation, God's activity on earth has not been by His Spirit alone, or by His Word alone, but by His Spirit and Word working together. At the beginning of Genesis, we read:

> *The Spirit of God was hovering over the face of the waters. Then God said...."*   (Genesis 1:2–3)

When the Word and the Spirit were combined, creation took place. And this is how God continues to work in our lives today—by the combination of His Word and His Spirit.

How is the love of God brought to perfection in us? By our keeping His Word. So again, it is not by the Spirit alone, nor by the Word alone, but rather by the Spirit working with the Word that God's love is poured out and then perfected in us.

6

UPWARD PROGRESS

With this chapter, we conclude part one, "Loving Others," of *The Coming Revival*. The vital question we asked at the beginning of this section was, "What does God require of us in order to bring revival to the church and to the nations?" We have discovered that His requirement is *love*. Only a God who *is* love would come up with that kind of requirement!

STEPS TO SPIRITUAL MATURITY

Before we move on to part two, "Loving God," I want to examine one of my favorite passages from 2 Peter, which speaks of our progress in the Christian life—the upbuilding of our spiritual character. The climax of this process is love. But there are six steps to reaching it after the initial step of faith:

> But also for this very reason, giving all diligence, add to your faith **virtue** [**excellence**], to virtue **knowledge**, to knowledge **self-control**, to self-control **perseverance**, to perseverance **godliness**, to godliness **brotherly kindness**, and to brotherly kindness **love**.
>
> (2 Peter 1:5–7)

Thus, the basis of every forward step in the Christian life is faith—but to our faith we are to add seven successive stages of character development.

STEP 1: VIRTUE

The first stage is *"virtue"*:

But also for this very reason, giving all diligence, add to your faith virtue [excellence].

I prefer to translate *"virtue"* as "excellence," which is one of its connotations in the original Greek. *Virtue* is a very broad word that has many meanings. For instance, you could say the virtue of a horse is to run fast. So, "excellence" is a good word to express the thought here.

I always like to emphasize that one of the first evidences in your life that you have been saved, in addition to loving others, is a desire to become excellent. If you were a teacher before you were saved, you should become an excellent teacher. If you were a bus driver, you should become an excellent bus driver. If you were a doctor or a dentist, you should become an excellent doctor or dentist. Excellence should be the mark of the Christian.

STEP 2: KNOWLEDGE

Add…to [excellence] *knowledge.*

I don't believe *"knowledge"* here is primarily meant to be scientific or intellectual understanding, but rather the knowledge of God's will revealed through His Word. We need that knowledge to progress in our Christian life and character.

STEP 3: SELF-CONTROL

To knowledge self-control.

"*Self-control*" is a character quality that is very rarely talked about in contemporary Christianity. However, if we do not develop this trait, we will not progress any further in our spiritual development. Why? Because every time we are about to move forward, we will lose control of ourselves and be defeated.

We have all experienced something like this. We are making progress, but then we might lose our temper or yield to lust, excessive appetites, negative emotions, hopelessness, or unbelief. Any of these can hinder our progress. That is why self-control is such an essential step in the total process of building Christian character.

STEP 4: PERSEVERANCE

To self-control perseverance [endurance].

Perseverance is another essential ingredient. In the process of maturing, you will encounter tests, trials, and obstacles. If you haven't acquired perseverance, or endurance, you will give up. And when you give up, your progress ceases.

At one point in her life, my wife Ruth was going through a significant struggle for her health. Every time one malady got better, something else got worse. Then she read a passage in James that begins,

> *My brethren, count it all joy when you fall into various trials....*
> (James 1:2)

When she read this, she felt the Holy Spirit convicting her: "You're sinning; you're disobeying the Word of God. You're not considering it all joy."

The passage in James goes on to say this:

> *...knowing that the testing of your faith produces patience* ["perseverance," or "endurance," NKJV marginal note]. *But let patience have its perfect work, that you may be perfect* ["mature," NKJV marginal note] *and complete, lacking nothing.* (James 1:3–4)

Do you want to be *"perfect and complete, lacking nothing"*? Then you have to cultivate perseverance. There is no other way. Otherwise, every time God puts you into a process that is designed to make you mature and complete, you will give up—and your progress will be halted.

These two traits, self-control and perseverance (or endurance), are what I call "the bottleneck." If you can't get through them, you can't make any further progress toward maturity.

Following self-control and perseverance, we get to some really great character qualities.

STEP 5: GODLINESS

…to perseverance godliness.

My definition of *godliness* is "a temperament controlled by the Holy Spirit." If you have the trait of godliness, all your reactions and responses are controlled by God's Spirit. The mark of godly people is that when they enter a room, God enters with them. They carry His presence wherever they go.

STEP 6: BROTHERLY KINDNESS

…to godliness brotherly kindness.

If you have the characteristic of brotherly kindness, you love your fellow believers deeply, or *"fervently,"* as Peter wrote in 1 Peter 1:22. Some of us still have not reached this sixth step! I have to confess that not all Christians are easy to love. I think I am probably one of them. Some people have come to me and said, concerning something that occurred years earlier, "Brother Prince, I have to forgive you for something." Other people have approached me and declared, "You've changed a lot!" Unfortunately, in both cases, I understood what they meant, and I had to acknowledge it was true.

However, brotherly kindness—as important as it is—is not the final step. There is one more quality we must attain.

STEP 7: AGAPE LOVE

In Greek, the name of the type of love that crowns the process of character development is *agape*. This refers to a type of love which loves those who don't understand you, loves those who are different from you, loves your enemies, loves your persecutors. Agape love is the climax of the Christian life—it is the very pinnacle.

A PROCESS OF GROWTH

It is clear that growth into spiritual maturity is a process. As we discussed at the end of the last chapter, there are two agents God uses in this process: the Holy Spirit and the Word of God. Even though we might have wonderful, individual spiritual experiences, we still must go through this development process. I have read the lives of missionaries and others who had wonderful spiritual experiences. Hudson Taylor, for example, the great missionary to China, had a glorious experience when he was filled with the love of God. Yet he had many personal problems, and he wasn't always easy to live with. He was a great man of God. But, like the rest of us, he had to go through this process of spiritual growth. No one is exempt. There is no other route to maturity than God's appointed way.

Let's review this process one more time: to your faith, add excellence; to excellence, add knowledge; to knowledge, add self-control; to self-control, add perseverance, or endurance; to perseverance, add godliness; to godliness, add brotherly kindness (love of your fellow believers); and to brotherly kindness, add love (*agape*). Love is the pinnacle. Love is the goal. Love is the destination for every Spirit-filled believer.

REMOVING THE BARRIERS

As we bring this section of the book to a close, it may be that you want to respond to what the Lord has been speaking to you so you can move forward in spiritual maturity. You may feel that there are various barriers in your way. I have learned by my own personal experience that unconfessed sin can be a major barrier to God's blessing. There are other barriers, but that is the number one, the most serious, and the most common barrier.

Most Christians know 1 John 1:9, *"If we confess our sins, He is faithful and just to forgive us our sins and to cleanse us from all unrighteousness."* However, many don't seem to realize there is an *"if"* in this verse. You may interpret the Bible differently from me, but I do not find that God has ever committed Himself to forgive a sin that has not been confessed.

Therefore, if we want our sins to be forgiven, what do we have to do? Confess them to God. Are you willing? It may be difficult and painful, but it is a step you can decide to take.

Please don't start to analyze or probe into yourself about your sins, because the further you probe, the worse you will feel. Let the Holy Spirit do it. Let God put His finger on every area in your life that you need to confess.

Many times, I have had to confess that I have not loved as I should have loved. I have often been critical, self-righteous, judgmental, self-centered, and insensitive. When I think back to the years when I helped to raise twelve children (with my first wife, Lydia, and then my second wife, Ruth), what I regret most is my insensitivity. I was an only child, with no brothers or sisters. So, growing up on my own, I learned to live my life my own way. It has taken me years to arrive at the point where, for example, I am even aware that somebody else doesn't feel well.

I have also learned this truth: when people have come up to ask me a theological question, usually, it was not a theological answer they really wanted. They wanted comfort. They wanted acceptance. A question about "theology" was just a way of saying, "Help me—I need to be loved."

I have confessed my lack of love to you, here in these pages, because I want to ask God to forgive me. If I don't confess, I know He will not forgive. If I do confess, I believe He will forgive. And I want you to take the same step—just between you and the Lord.

I invite you to join me in the following prayer of confession, or you can pray in your own words. Let us acknowledge that we haven't been as loving as we should have been. Then, let us ask God to pour out His love on us in a new dimension. We will ask for a revival of love in our hearts.

Lord, I want to confess before You now, as Your believing child, that I have failed You. I have misrepresented You. I have given the world the wrong impression of the kind of people Your children are. I have not caused them to know I am Your disciple because I have not loved others the way You have commanded me to. I have often been self-righteous, self-centered, critical, and condemnatory. I want to acknowledge my failure before You. I have sinned. I have broken the first and greatest of all commandments, to love You, the Lord my God, with all my heart, soul, and mind. And I have broken the second commandment because I haven't loved my neighbor as myself. All I can do is say I am sorry. Please forgive me and change my heart. Send Your Holy Spirit to do in me and for me what only You can do.

And now, Lord, on the basis of Your forgiveness as I have humbled myself before You, I ask You to pour out Your love upon me in a new measure, to a new degree. Please open a fountain of love in my heart that will flow out into the lives of the people around me who are longing for love. They are not looking for religion—they are looking for love. And You have chosen me to be a vessel and channel of Your love. Start with me, Lord. Do whatever needs to be done to change me. I pray all this in the name of Jesus. Amen.

PART TWO:
LOVING GOD

7

TWO INSEPARABLE REALITIES

In part one, "Loving Others," we learned many biblical truths about love: love is the fulfillment of the law, the outworking of righteousness, the debt we owe one another, the aim of our Christian instruction, the greatest spiritual gift, and the ultimate quality. In fact, the entire goal of God's purpose for our lives is love. If we deviate from this goal and miss it, we will miss everything that is important for us as Christians—including our part in bringing revival to the world. We must learn how to love others if we are to play a role in the coming revival.

Now, in part two, "Loving God," we will search the Scriptures to find answers to our next essential question for revival: What does it mean to love God?

LOVE AND OBEDIENCE

In a portion of Scripture we looked at earlier, Jesus taught us the most important commandments of all:

> You shall love the LORD your God with all your heart, with all your soul, and with all your mind." This is the first and great commandment. And the second is like it: "You shall love your neighbor as yourself." On these two commandments hang all the Law and the Prophets.
>
> (Matthew 22:37–40)

Since loving God is the foremost commandment, how do we whole-heartedly love Him? Right from the beginning, we must understand this truth: love for God can never be separated from *obedience* to Him. The love of God is not mushy, sentimental, or purely emotional. It carries deep emotion with it—but it is rooted in the *will*, not in the *emotions*.

THE RIGHT MOTIVATION

Jesus often talked about love with His disciples. He even did so in His last hours with them prior to His death. Let us look at four verses in John 19 that are part of Jesus's final instructions to the twelve disciples before His crucifixion. We will begin with verse 21:

> *He who has My commandments and keeps them [or obeys them], it is he who loves Me. And he who loves Me will be loved by My Father, and I will love him and manifest Myself to him.* (John 14:21)

With these words, Jesus was giving us two important insights. First, our motivation for obeying God should be love, not fear. Second, genuine love for God is expressed by obedience. This bears repeating, because it is fundamental in the Christian life: the motive for obeying God is love, and love is expressed by obedience to Him.

FEAR OR LOVE?

Unfortunately, there are many Christians who serve God more out of fear of Him than out of love for Him. Let's consider for a moment what Paul says about fear in Romans 8:15: *"For you did not receive the spirit of bondage again to fear, but you received the Spirit of adoption by whom we cry out, 'Abba, Father.'"* Paul is referring to the law of Moses. The Jews obeyed the law because they were afraid of the consequences of disobedience. But, in the new covenant, the motive for obedience is love, not fear.

The difference between these two approaches can be seen in the raising of children. I am not speaking theoretically because, as I mentioned previously, I helped to raise twelve children. I have definitely had my share of experience! Essentially, there are two ways to bring up children. You can make a lot of rules and strictly enforce them—basically controlling your children through fear. Or, you can raise your children in an atmosphere of love and trust.

If your children are motivated to obey out of fear, then, when they reach their teenage years, they will rebel against your rules. They will leave home as soon as they can and go their own way. However, if you win their hearts, they will be motivated by love for you and will continue to follow what you have taught them well into adulthood. Love is the only effective motivation for obedience.

This is exactly what Jesus is saying in John 14:21 when He makes the statement, *"He who has My commandments and keeps them, it is he who loves Me."* Please notice that in order to keep the commandments, you must first "have" the commandments. In other words, you need to seek out God's will. We cannot have a passive, resigned attitude that says, "Well, if the Bible says so, I guess I will have to do it." God is looking for a deeper personal relationship with us than that. He wants us to seek His will out of love for Him—and then obey Him, because His ways are true and right.

"WE WILL COME"

Judas (not Iscariot) said to Him, "Lord, how is it that You will manifest Yourself to us, and not to the world?"   (John 14:22)

Judas asked this question because earlier in John 14, Jesus had told His disciples He was going away. He said He would be leaving them, but He would come back and communicate with them again.

Jesus answered and said to him, "If anyone loves Me, he will keep My word; and My Father will love him, and We will come to him and make Our home with him."   (John 14:23)

This is a very special verse. It is one of the few places in the New Testament—or in the whole Bible, for that matter—where the plural pronoun is used of God. It is rare. Jesus does not say, "I will come," but *"We will come."* The Father, the Son, and the Spirit will all come to make their home with the one who keeps the Word of God. What an amazing promise!

THE MEASURE OF OUR LOVE

In the next verse, Jesus states the opposite truth:

> *He who does **not** love Me does not keep My words; and the word which*
> *you hear is not Mine but the Father's who sent Me.*   (John 14:24)

Do you want to know how much you love God? You can easily find out. It is exactly how much you obey His Word. You do not love Him any more than you obey His commandments. You may say you love Him, you may pray as if you love Him, and you may do many good works to show you love Him. But the true measure of your love is the measure of your *obedience* to His Word.

Thus, love is both the motivation and the evidence of our obedience. This truth could frighten each of us. I could ask myself, "If I'm not totally obedient, does it mean I don't love God?"

The answer is no. In the Christian life, growth in love and obedience is progressive. When you become a Christian, you don't start out by completely obeying everything. In fact, I have lived the Christian life for over sixty years, and there are still a lot of areas in which I don't fully know, understand, and follow the will of God. We can take encouragement from Philippians 1:6: *"Being confident of this very thing, that He who has begun a good work in you will complete it until the day of Jesus Christ."*

HOLD ON TO YOUR FAITH

In the book of Romans, Paul says this about Abraham, the father of our faith:

> *For what does the Scripture say? "Abraham believed God, and it was*
> *accounted to him for righteousness."*   (Romans 4:3)

Paul is quoting from Genesis 15:6, where it says Abraham's faith was accounted to him as righteousness because he believed the promise of God. If you read the full account of the life of Abraham in Genesis, you will discover there are at least two occasions where he totally missed God's will. On the first occasion, he let his wife, Sarah, be taken into an Egyptian pharaoh's harem as a concubine. (See Genesis 12:14–20.) On the second occasion, he agreed to Sarah's suggestion to have a son by her maidservant, Hagar. (See Genesis 16:1–2.)

In each case, Abraham missed God. He did not perfectly follow the will of God. However—and this is indeed good news—even when he wasn't totally obedient, his faith was *"accounted to him for righteousness."*

Abraham is our pattern in this. At the end of Romans 4, Paul wrote:

> *Now it was not written for* [Abraham's] *sake alone that it was imputed to him, but also for us. It shall be imputed to us who believe in Him who raised up Jesus our Lord from the dead.* (Romans 4:23–24)

As long as we continue to believe, remaining in faith, as long as our hearts are set to obey and follow God, our faith is still accounted to us for righteousness—even when we are not fully obeying, and even when we miss the way for a time. It is very important for us to grasp this truth. Please don't let the devil bring you under condemnation if you are not always totally obedient. Many times, you might stumble and fall. But follow Abraham's example. He stumbled, he made mistakes, but he never gave up. In spite of his errors, his faith was always accounted to him for righteousness.

I am reminded of the dialogue between Jesus and Peter at the Last Supper. Jesus said to him:

> *"Simon, Simon! Indeed, Satan has asked for you, that he may sift you as wheat. But I have prayed for you, that your faith should not fail; and when you have returned to Me, strengthen your brethren." But he said to Him, "Lord, I am ready to go with You, both to prison and to death." Then He said, "I tell you, Peter, the rooster shall not crow this day before you will deny three times that you know Me."* (Luke 22:31–34)

Jesus was saying, "Peter, even if you are attacked by Satan, and even if you deny me three times, it will be all right in the end—provided you don't let go of your faith."

So, hold on to your faith. No matter how weak you are, no matter how many times you stumble, no matter how unworthy you may feel—don't give up your faith. Why? Because your faith is accounted to you for righteousness. If you hold on to your faith, just as Jesus brought Peter through, He will bring you through. Our faith is not in ourselves—it is in His faithfulness.

8

PROGRESSIVE OBEDIENCE

We have established that in the Christian life, obedience is progressive. When we first receive Christ, we don't start out by perfectly loving and obeying God. Like most endeavors we undertake in life, we make progress over time, step-by-step. In this chapter, I would like to share some of my own experiences with "progressive obedience."

A SERVICE IN YORKSHIRE

In 1941, almost by accident, I stumbled into a Pentecostal church in Yorkshire, England. At the time, I didn't know there were such people as Pentecostals. As a matter of fact, I don't think I had even heard of Baptists. I knew there were Anglicans because I had grown up in that denomination. I knew there were Roman Catholics, and I knew there were people called Methodists who had made "trouble" previously in British history. But that was about the limit of my knowledge of denominations.

I went to the Pentecostal service in Yorkshire only because a fellow soldier invited me. I knew it was a church service by the apologetic way he said, "Would you like to come somewhere with me on Sunday afternoon?" I said to him, "Well, I should tell you I don't believe in religion. But I've got nothing better to do on Sunday afternoon, so I'll come just to see." I had no idea what I would see—and I definitely saw much more than I expected!

During my seven years at the University of Cambridge, I had been trained intellectually to criticize and analyze everything. As a result, I had a skeptical attitude, which was the basis for the one question I considered as I entered this church service: "Does this preacher really know what he's talking about?"

The preacher's text was from Isaiah 6, where the prophet Isaiah had the vision of the Lord in His glory and radiance. When Isaiah saw the Lord in His glory, he said, *"Woe is me, for I am undone! Because I am a man of unclean lips, and I dwell in the midst of a people of unclean lips"* (verse 5).

When I heard the phrase "a man of unclean lips dwelling in the midst of a people of unclean lips," I said to myself, "No one ever described me more accurately than that." With all due respect for the British army, I don't think there is any group of men anywhere in the world who excelled more in unclean speech and blasphemy. I had been in the army long enough to know I was as bad as the rest of the men.

Before I proceed with this story, I have to add that if you had been planning to convince a philosopher from Cambridge about Christianity, you wouldn't have used that particular meeting. First of all, the preacher got lost several times in his message, wandering around in a lot of details unrelated to the passage in Isaiah. At some point, he was talking about the relationship between David the shepherd boy and Saul the king. When he said (quite rightly) that Saul was head and shoulders taller than the rest of the people, he got very involved in an imaginary dialogue between Saul and David. For dramatic effect, when he was speaking as David, he stood on the platform, but when he was speaking as Saul, he stood up on a little bench on the platform and looked down at where he had stood when he was acting the part of David.

Well, in the middle of one sequence in which he was playing Saul, the bench collapsed and he fell to the ground with a loud thud! So, as I said, if you had been planning to convince a sophisticated Cambridge intellectual about Christianity, you would have left that part out of it.

But at the end of it all, I came to one simple conclusion about this preacher: "He knows what he is talking about—and I don't."

A MIRACLE

After this, the preacher took me by surprise and actually embarrassed me. He made what is commonly called "an appeal" for salvation. In those days, they used no background music for an altar call, just the request for "every head bowed, every eye closed." As I understood it, the people at this church were saying, "If you want this thing, put your hand up." Well, I couldn't figure out what "this thing" was, except for what had happened to Isaiah. So I sat there, paralyzed and embarrassed, and thought to myself, "I've never been in a church where anybody asked me to do something so undignified as to put my hand up in public."

But as I sat there in what seemed to be a very long silence, two inaudible voices were speaking to me. One of them said, "You are a soldier in uniform. If you put your hand up in front of all these old ladies, you're going to look very silly." The other voice said, "If this is something good, why shouldn't you have it?"

Honestly, I was paralyzed. I couldn't respond. And then a miracle took place. A real miracle, and it happened to me. I saw my own right arm go up in the air—and I knew I had not raised it!

Well, that was all the people there had been were waiting for, and they went right back to the rest of the service. I didn't receive any counseling or further instruction, but I had raised my hand.

THE IMPASSE

Two nights later, I was in another Pentecostal meeting, and I thought, "I'm going to see this through." It was in a different church, with a different preacher, but otherwise, it was very much the same. This man preached on Genesis 5:24: *"Enoch...was not, for God took him."*

Now, he was another of these preachers who believed in taking creative license. He described how, in search of the missing Enoch, the local army's "special investigative branch" called in their tracking dogs. The dogs followed Enoch's scent just so far, and then the scent disappeared. The preacher said, "The scent didn't go north, it didn't go south, it didn't go east, and it didn't go west—Enoch must have gone up." I said to myself, "That's logical. I can accept that."

So, this time when they made the appeal, I was ready. I knew what was going to happen. I thought to myself, "Somebody else put my hand up for me the last time, and I can't expect that to happen twice—so I'll put my hand up." And I did.

The preacher came over to me and gave me a little more attention than the previous one had. However, he looked at me for a moment as if he thought he had a problem on his hands. Then, he asked me two questions. The first one was, "Do you believe you are a sinner?"

Now, my academic specialty had been definitions. So I quickly ran through my mind all the obvious definitions of a sinner, and every one of them fitted me exactly. So I said, "Yes, I believe I'm a sinner." Then he said, "Do you believe Christ died for your sins?" To this day, I remember exactly what I replied: "To tell you the truth, I can't see what the death of Jesus Christ nineteen centuries ago could have to do with the sins I've committed in my lifetime."

And there I was—at an impasse. I think he was wise enough not to argue with me, and I am sure those dear Pentecostal people began to pray for me. In that church, they had actually had what they called a "revival," but there was only one person who had responded—and it was me! So they had every reason to pray for me.

I wasn't saved that night. I felt I had stepped out of one world, but I had not yet stepped into another. I was like a person suspended between two worlds. I went on in this way from Monday to Thursday. During this time, there were three questions in my mind. The first one was, "If I get involved in this, what will happen to my university career?" The second one was, "What will my friends say?" And the third, "What will my family say?" That was the hardest question of all. But by Thursday, I came to this conclusion: "I don't care what happens to my university career, I don't care what my friends say, and I don't care what my family says. Whatever this is, I want it." And that night, I took the definitive step. I was gloriously saved in my army barracks room. God knows when you are totally prepared to receive Him.

SLOW AND STEADY PROGRESS

Earlier, I referred to my awareness of my unclean speech. Amazingly, the moment God saved me and filled me with the Holy Spirit, my tongue was cleansed. I never used another unclean or blasphemous word. It wasn't through my own effort—it just was no longer in me. I thought, "That's wonderful! I've arrived." Then, God began to show me the many other ways in which we can sin with our tongues. After a while, He convicted me of being very critical of people, telling me, "What right have you to judge other people's lives?" So I gave up being critical.

After a considerable period of time (note that this didn't all happen in a few weeks), God convicted me that I frequently used negative speech. I would often speak in terms of unbelief rather than belief. In a way, when I did this, I was giving more glory to the devil than to the Lord. I wasn't trusting in God's grace and power. God dealt with this tendency in my life by leading me to the words of Jesus in Matthew 5:37:

> But let your "Yes" be "Yes," and your "No," "No." For whatever is more than these is from the evil one.

This was a breathtaking statement to me. I saw that, as a Christian, I was obligated to say what I meant. No more, no less. No exaggeration. No varnishing of the story, just simply telling it like it is.

James says if any man can control his tongue, he is a perfect man. (See James 3:2.) Would you agree with this conclusion? I certainly do!

What I have described above is an account of my progress. But attaining it has taken me years. I don't claim to have arrived, and my obedience has been step-by-step. It has been a process. Yet even in those times when my obedience was incomplete, my faith was accounted to me for righteousness. I hope my testimony helps you, because so many Christians come under condemnation in their efforts to be perfect. They fail, they make a mistake, they commit a sin, and they think, "It's all over. God is finished with me." But that is not true—not as long as you hold on to your faith. Jesus did not say to Peter, "I prayed that you wouldn't deny Me three times." He said, "I prayed that your faith would not fail."

WHAT ABOUT YOU?

Perhaps, as you have read this chapter, you have realized you are struggling with feelings of failure or condemnation. If so, I want to lead you in a prayer that will bring you relief and confidence. Our enemy, Satan, is the adversary of our souls. The Scriptures call him "the accuser of the brethren." (See Revelation 12:10.) If you are in a battle with the accuser, please pray this prayer out loud with me now:

> Dear Lord Jesus, Abraham made mistakes, but his faith was still *"accounted to him for righteousness."* You prayed for Peter that his faith would not fail, knowing that Satan would soon "sift" him, and he would deny You. I, too, have failed. But I am not giving up. Like Abraham and Peter, I am trusting that my faith will be "accounted to me for righteousness."
>
> I stand in faith against the condemnation of the accuser, holding fast to Your Word in 1 John 1:9: *"If we confess our sins, He is faithful and just to forgive us our sins and to cleanse us from all unrighteousness."* I humbly come to You in sorrow over my sins, which I confess to You now [name the sins that are troubling you].
>
> No matter how I have stumbled, I trust You, Lord Jesus, to bring me through—and I thank You in advance for helping me to move forward. I will hold on to my faith and trust You to keep me going by Your faithfulness. In Jesus's name. Amen.

9

OUR JEALOUS GOD

As we seek to understand what it truly means to love God, we need to consider a particular aspect of His character that may disturb us: the "jealousy" of God.

RESERVED FOR HIM

God is jealous. His love is a jealous love. Many people don't like to hear this because they think of jealousy in a negative light. The Bible teaches that there is a type of jealousy that is sinful—the kind that is self-centered, ambitious, and controlling. (See, for example, 2 Corinthians 12:20; Galatians 5:20.) However, there is also a pure type of jealousy, a godly jealousy, one that is related to holiness and agape love.

God's jealousy falls into this category. It occurs when those whom He deeply loves and who are a part of Him ignore or forsake Him. To me, it is almost incredible that Almighty God, the Creator of the universe, would care so much about a person like me that He would be jealous if my heart turned in any direction but to Him! It is amazing—but it is true. God is a jealous God.

In the Ten Commandments, as they are presented in Exodus 20:4–5, God makes these statements:

You shall not make for yourself a carved image—any likeness of anything that is in heaven above, or that is in the earth beneath, or that is in the water under the earth; you shall not bow down to them nor serve them. For I, the LORD your God, am a jealous God.

Then, in Exodus 34:14, God restates this idea: "*You shall worship no other god, for the LORD, whose name is Jealous, is a jealous God.*" In other words, God was saying, "I don't want any other person or object to take the place reserved for Me."

I am a logician, and after reading God's Word, I have come face-to-face with this fact: if Almighty God—in all His majesty, glory, power, and wisdom—is willing to come into my life, then logically there is only one place in my life I can offer Him: first place. To offer God second or third place is to insult the Almighty. I am afraid many of us have been guilty of doing that.

GENUINE DISCIPLES

In the New Testament, Jesus says some disturbing words that seem to echo the declaration of God's jealousy we just read in Exodus. Although these are very troubling statements, each of us must grapple with them. (Let me say again that if you have never been shocked by something you have read in the Bible, I doubt whether you have ever really read it. It is a disturbing book, and it was designed to disturb us.) Here is the first of those statements:

Now great multitudes went with Him. And He turned and said to them, "If anyone comes to Me and does not hate his father and mother, wife and children, brothers and sisters, yes, and his own life also, he cannot be My disciple." (Luke 14:25–26)

What attitude did Jesus exhibit toward those multitudes? Did He say, "Isn't it wonderful I have a great company of followers?" No. In fact, in a certain sense, He did everything He could to discourage them from following Him.

Today, many believers tend to admire megachurches. They like to know which is the biggest church in the world and the second biggest—congregations with hundreds of thousands of members. I don't believe Jesus is impressed by the numbers of people in megachurches, because He did not tell us to make *church members*. What did He tell us to do? He said, *"Go therefore and **make disciples** of all the nations"* (Matthew 28:19).

There is a significant difference between a church member and a disciple. A disciple is someone whose primary aim in life is to follow Jesus. In contrast, a church member might be someone who is merely "religious" or has a respect for Jesus—someone who attends church services and leads a "good" life. I believe one of Christianity's biggest problems is that there are too many church members who are *not* disciples.

To illustrate this point, let me share with you a rather unusual story. I know of a woman who was a communist, a lesbian, and a violent, militant feminist. She was actually buying revolvers for the purpose of shooting men. Somehow, she became involved in a nefarious scheme with two of her associates, and they ended up on a small ship in the China Sea. The weather began to turn bad, and the people who were with her said, "Go down into the hold, switch on the radio, and see what the weather report is."

She went down into the hold, turned on the radio, and heard my radio program broadcasting from Manila in the Philippines—and she was wonderfully saved! This is amazing to me, because my messages are no more than twelve-and-a-half minutes long. She was totally transformed, and she devoted her life to winning to the Lord people of the same persuasion she had been before she was saved.

She became a true disciple. However, she had one problem: the people whom she led to the Lord also became true disciples. How could this be a problem? When she took them to church, the people in the church were much less committed to what they believed than she and her friends were. As a result, these new believers couldn't feel at home in the church. Lukewarm church members can become a barrier to the spreading of the gospel.

THE CALL TO DISCIPLESHIP

In the book of Revelation, Jesus said to the church of Laodicea, "*You are neither cold nor hot. I could wish you were cold or hot.... You are luke-warm*" (Revelation 3:15–16). If you are spiritually cold, you don't deceive anybody—you do not call yourself a Christian or make any professions of faith. If you are spiritually hot, you challenge people to become disciples. But if you are lukewarm, you mislead people. Why? Because you give them a wrong impression of what Christianity really is. In Revelation, Jesus went on to say one of the most offensive statements He could make: "*Because you are lukewarm,...I will vomit you out of My mouth*" (Revelation 3:16). Do you believe the Lord would speak like that? Whether you like or not, He did. The Lord is very plainspoken.

God is not interested in our making more church members unless they become disciples as well. Once again, when Jesus saw the multitudes, He didn't say, "Come on and join Me! We're going to have a wonderful time. You're going to get wonderfully blessed!" He said something quite differ-ent. He challenged them with a call to discipleship. Let's read it again:

> If anyone comes to Me and does not hate his father and mother, wife and children, brothers and sisters, yes, and his own life also, he cannot be My disciple.   (Luke 14:26)

This is a very searching statement, to say the least. Is Jesus really asking us to hate our family members? No, He is not. But even our family mem-bers cannot become a barrier to our love for Him. They must not take the place in our hearts and lives that He claims for Himself alone. He says, "In that case, you must have an attitude of 'hatred' toward them. You must 'hate' *anything* that takes My place in your life." Jesus was also careful to say we must hate our own lives as well if we are to follow Him.

SELF-LOVE

What Jesus is saying in these verses may sound severe. But He knows it is the only antidote to the spirit of this age, which is self-love. In 2 Timothy 3:2–5, Paul gives a list of eighteen different moral blemishes that will afflict humanity at the close of the age. Almost all of them are conspicuous in today's culture.

First on Paul's list is the tendency for people to be *"lovers of themselves."* I have come to see that the greatest single problem in the Christian life is likewise self-love. It breaks up marriages and families because self-love says, "If you don't suit me, you can go. It's true we got married, but if you can't get along with me and my way of doing things, then you can leave."

Thus, self-love is the root of the breakup of the family, which is the root of the breakup of society. But Jesus says, "When it comes to your relationship to Me, you have to 'hate' yourself, your father, your mother, your brothers, your sisters, and your spouse." That is a radical statement! Again, please understand this does not mean it is right to hate people. It means you must purge yourself of anything that comes between Jesus and you—anything that takes the place of Jesus in your life. He demands that you eliminate it from the place of priority it occupies. Only Jesus can take first place.

TAKING UP OUR CROSS

In Luke 14:27, Jesus goes on to say,

And whoever does not bear his cross and come after Me cannot be My disciple.

I have heard two definitions of the cross, in the above context, that I think are worth mentioning. Here is the first: "The cross in your life is where God's will and your will cross." At that point, you have to make a decision: will you yield to God's will even though it differs from your own? Here is the second definition: "The cross is the place where you die." You don't have to take up the cross. It is voluntary. But if you do take it up, you will have to die to "self." Unless you meet these conditions, Jesus said, "[You] *cannot be My disciple.*"

It is impossible to be a disciple of Jesus and let anyone or anything else take the place in your life He claims. He is jealous. He will not share that position with any other person, activity, or thing. In Luke 14:33, Jesus says,

So likewise, whoever of you does not forsake all that he has cannot be My disciple.

Please take note: Jesus does not say, "...may not be My disciple" or "... will find it difficult to be My disciple." In each of the three verses from Luke 14 we have reviewed—verses 26, 27, and 33—Jesus explicitly says, "...*cannot be My disciple.*" In other words, if there is anything you are clutching and will not relinquish for the sake of Jesus, you cannot be His disciple. This doesn't necessarily mean you have to give away all your possessions. (That is the requirement Jesus made of one young man in the New Testament. We will look at his story in the next chapter.) What it means for you is this: you have to release anything in your life more important to you than loving and obeying Jesus.

10

THE ONE BARRIER

Please allow me to share a very personal illustration that relates to the topic with which we concluded the previous chapter—the cost of genuine discipleship. As we discovered, sometimes God asks us to let go of everything. That is essentially what happened to me.

GIVING ALL FOR JESUS

I have mentioned my service with the British army in North Africa. Later, I was sent to Palestine, and at that time, I believed God had specifically called me to serve Him there. When the time came for my discharge from the army at the end of the war, the army owed me passage back to England. It was my right, and they were obligated to get me home. But as I was making preparations to go, God prompted me to pray in tongues, and then He immediately provided the interpretation. It said, in effect, "The ship is in the harbor, the sails are up, and everything is ready. If you get on board now, you can go. If you miss it now, you will never go."

I knew I had no option but to obey God. He was telling me to remain in Palestine. At that time, my dear grandfather, to whom I was closer than any other member of my family, was dying of cancer. I was his only grandson. He longed to see me, and I longed to see him. But I had to say no. I had to give it up.

In a similar vein, around the same time, King's College in Cambridge, which was my college, wrote me a very flattering letter. They informed me that if I would come back, I would have an assured academic career in one of the most distinguished academic institutions in Britain, with all the attending benefits. I had to write them back with my answer. (I was not tactful in my response, and I would not do it the same way again.) I said, "I can't come. I have become a Christian."

So, I gave up my family, my country, and my career. In addition, my first wife, Lydia, and I had to buy a house in order to save our lives (I won't take the time to go into the details here). The only way we could do that was for me to use my life savings.

God did not say to me, "You cannot be My disciple unless you give up everything." He just brought about the circumstances that caused me to do it. Only afterward did I realize I had fulfilled the conditions of discipleship. I am not suggesting that God will deal with you in exactly the same way, but His conditions remain the same. We must give up anything He asks us to. Anyone who is not willing to forsake all that he has for Jesus Christ cannot be His disciple.

A COSTLY INVITATION

That is my personal story. Now, let's turn to an account in the book of Mark that describes Jesus's encounter with a young man—and the barrier that kept this young man from becoming a disciple of Jesus. This story has made a deep impression on me over the years.

> Now as [Jesus] *was going out on the road, one came running, knelt before Him, and asked Him, "Good Teacher, what shall I do that I may inherit eternal life?"*   (Mark 10:17)

Later in Mark's account, we discover that this individual who came to Jesus was a wealthy young ruler. Here, it says he *"came running"* to Jesus— he was enthusiastic.

> *So Jesus said to him, "Why do you call Me good? No one is good but One, that is, God. You know the commandments: 'Do not commit adultery,'*

'Do not murder,' 'Do not steal,' 'Do not bear false witness,' 'Do not de-
fraud,' 'Honor your father and your mother.'" And he answered and said
to Him [I am sure he was speaking the truth], *"Teacher, all these things*
I have kept from my youth." [He was a very good, moral, upright young
man.] *Then Jesus, looking at him, loved him....*   (Mark 10:18–21)

The phrase *"Jesus, looking at him, loved him"* is arresting to me. I think I
can say this: it is frightening to be loved by Jesus. When He loves you, He
looks at you and sees right into the innermost depths of your personality.
He knows everything about you, and He will unerringly put His finger on
the one barrier that stands between you and Him.

This barrier is not the same for everyone. With the young ruler, it was
his possessions. But with others, it could be something very different. For
instance, in your life, it could be an attachment to a girlfriend or boyfriend.
It could be a job you particularly aspired to and achieved or the pursuit of
an advanced academic degree. Whatever it is, if it is more important to you
than Jesus, He will bring it to your attention. And then you will need to
make a choice about your priorities in life.

Jesus, looking at him, loved him, and said to him, "One thing you
lack...."   (Mark 10:21)

The rich young man lacked only *"one thing"*—but it was the only truly
important aspect of life. Everything else was secondary. The young ruler
had everything life had to offer, except for this:

One thing you lack: Go your way, sell whatever you have and give to
the poor, and you will have treasure in heaven; and come, take up the
cross [notice this particular command], *and follow Me.*   (verse 21)

Let me repeat that Jesus did not place this condition on everybody who
came to Him. Nowhere in the New Testament does it say that when you
are saved, you have to give all your possessions to the poor (although I
respect those who have done that). Jesus put His finger on the one barrier
that came between that young man and his salvation or discipleship. He
said, "Just give up everything you own. Sell it all, and come and follow Me."

I appreciate how vivid the New Testament is in its descriptions. Remember that when this rich young ruler first came to Jesus, he *"came running"* (Mark 10:17). Yet when he left, he was walking:

> *But he was sad at this word, and went away sorrowful, for he had great possessions.*   (Mark 10:22)

Most people think having *"great possessions"* would make them happy. The opposite was the case for this young man. His great possessions made him unhappy. Why? Because he was not willing to let go of them in order to follow Jesus.

THE CHALLENGE

I want to close this chapter, as well as part two of this book, by issuing a challenge. For a moment, I want you to picture yourself standing alone with Jesus. Nobody else is in the picture. Jesus is looking at you, and He loves you. But with His loving eyes, He is looking into the innermost part of your personality. He knows everything about your past. He sees every aspect of your character. And He says, "In order to follow Me, you have to give up the one thing that is holding you back. You have to lay it at My feet."

I believe you might be in this position of needing to give up a barrier between you and Jesus. You might be a sincere Christian and a church member in good standing. You might do a lot of good things. Like that young man, you might keep all the commandments. But Jesus is saying to you, *"One thing you lack...."* Perhaps the one element you lack is the most important matter of all: a committed personal relationship with Jesus in which He is Lord over everything in your life. Or, maybe it a particular aspect of your life that you are grasping tightly and don't want to give up.

Please continue to think about this "one thing" question for a moment. If you have the sense that Jesus is confronting you—and I believe He may be doing just that—how will you respond? Will you lay everything at His feet without reservation and say, "Lord, please take me as I am. I will serve You and follow You to the best of my ability"? Or, will you say, "Lord, I'd really like to follow You fully, but [my girlfriend or boyfriend wouldn't understand; my family might not approve; I might lose my job; my friends would make fun of me]." Is there a "but" that stands between you and Jesus right now?

"One thing" is needed. Many activities in life are important or enjoyable—but only one matter is absolutely necessary: to become a fully committed disciple of Jesus Christ.

This could be the most critical moment of your entire life. You will probably never be in a better place or have a better time to make this decision than right now. Will you say this prayer with me?

> Lord Jesus, You gave up everything for me. You died for me so that I might be saved. I give myself to You now without reservation. I lay down everything in my life I have made more important than You. I submit myself and yield myself to You without reservation. No strings attached and no secret conditions. Unconditional surrender. Please receive me the way I am and make me what You want me to be. For Your glory, Lord Jesus. Amen.

Now you can freely thank God for His mercy and for what He is about to do in your life! Whatever His plan involves, you can depend upon Jesus to help you. He is the One who humbled Himself to accomplish the Father's will on earth. And that is the next step toward revival that we will examine: humbling ourselves.

PART THREE:

HUMBLING OURSELVES

11

THE ROOT OF THE PROBLEM

In this book, our primary goal is to open the way for worldwide revival. After decades of the church's extensive evangelistic efforts, intercessory prayer and fasting, and prophetic words and proclamations, the world continues to fall into greater and greater darkness. Where is the church's light, the *"city...set on a hill"* (Matthew 5:14)? The distressing state of the world and the church's ineffectiveness as an instrument of transformation are deep burdens on many believers today. You may carry those burdens as well.

WHAT DOES GOD REQUIRE?

As we commit ourselves to be part of the solution, our number-one question should be: "What does God require of us?" In parts one and two of this book, we talked about two foundational requirements for revival. The first priority is to love others. The Bible says we must *"make love [our] aim* (1 Corinthians 14:1 RSV)—before we even think about seeking spiritual gifts or other blessings. The Bible also says, *"The goal of our instruction is love"* (1 Timothy 1:5 NASB). If we diverge from this goal, our efforts will be aimless and fruitless. But if we make love our priority, it can be the key to revival.

An equal priority is to wholeheartedly love Jesus Christ—with the kind of love that leads to genuine discipleship. We concluded part two with a prayer of relinquishment, to let go of anything standing between us and Jesus. I hope you joined in that prayer, because this type of love is what Jesus demands of us.

In the next three parts of this book, we will deal with what I believe are primary hindrances to revival. The first hindrance can be summed up in one very short, unpopular word—*pride*.

Without question, I believe pride is the root problem in the church today. Not only is it a problem in the Western church, but it is increasingly a problem throughout the worldwide church. Over the course of my lifetime, I have ministered in over fifty nations around the world. I love the people of Great Britain, my homeland. I also love America and Israel, my adopted countries. But pride is a problem in each of those nations. In fact, this issue applies to the entire body of Christ in all nations of the world. The problem of pride is universal.

FULFILL GOD'S CONDITION

Our key Scripture for this part of our study is 2 Chronicles 7:14. This verse, familiar to most Christians, is a beautiful promise from God. I believe it is a promise of revival. The Lord begins by saying,

If My people who are called by My name....

If you are a Christian, you are called by the name of Christ. His is the name placed upon all of us as believers, and these words apply specifically to us. Here is the entire verse:

If My people who are called by My name will humble themselves, and pray and seek My face, and turn from their wicked ways, then I will hear from heaven, and will forgive their sin and heal their land.
                                                                    (2 Chronicles 7:14)

As I have taught on this verse over the decades, and in many different countries, and I have pointed out that there are seven distinct sections to it. There are four conditions for us to fulfill, and there are three promises

God makes if we fulfill those conditions. Here are the four conditions we need to fulfill as His people:

1. Humble ourselves

2. Pray

3. Seek His face

4. Turn from our wicked ways

Then, God gives us three promises:

1. I will hear from heaven.

2. I will forgive their sins.

3. I will heal their land.

While I have preached on 2 Chronicles 7:14 for many years, and even wrote a book based on this passage entitled *Shaping History Through Prayer and Fasting*,[2] God recently showed me something in this text I had never seen before—and it shocked and startled me. Here is what I understood Him to say: "In this generation, My people who are called by My name have never fulfilled the first condition." Without the first condition, all the other promises are empty. The first condition is, *"If My people…will humble themselves."*

If we wish to see the fulfillment of God's promise of revival, we must meet this condition of humbling ourselves.

THE HISTORY OF PRIDE

The first sin in the universe did not take place on earth, nor was it committed by a human being. It took place in heaven and was committed by an archangel, Lucifer. After Lucifer's rebellion and fall, his name became Satan, which means "the adversary" or "the accuser."

Before we examine a Scripture passage concerning the rebellion and fall of Satan, it is important for us to understand something about prophetic passages. One of the functions of prophesy is not merely to tell us what is *going to happen*, but also to give us information about what *has already happened* that we couldn't otherwise know. For instance, Moses was

---

2. For an updated and expanded edition of this book, see Derek Prince, *Shaping History Through Prayer and Fasting* (New Kensington, PA: Whitaker House, 2018).

a prophet, and he is the one who recorded the revelation in the book of Genesis of how creation took place. Without that revelation, we could never have known it. It was another prophet, Ezekiel, who poetically depicted for us the fall of Lucifer. His description is found in the twenty-eighth chapter of the book bearing his name. For our purposes, I will only touch on the main points of the passage.

In this biblical account, God addresses two distinct persons. The first person is *"the prince of Tyre."* (See Ezekiel 28:1–10.) The second person is *"the king of Tyre."* (See verses 11–19.) It is very clear that the prince of Tyre is a regular human being. It is equally clear that the king of Tyre (who has influence over the prince of Tyre) is not a human being. This passage brings out a very important fact, especially for understanding spiritual warfare. Human, earthly kingdoms are sometimes ruled by satanic spiritual kingdoms in the heavenlies. We can see the outworking of this principle throughout history.

SATANIC INFLUENCE

If we really want to address the problems in our world, it is not sufficient for us to deal with them on their earthly level. We have to address them on the heavenly level—and there is only one company of people equipped and armed to do that. It is not the politicians. It is not the generals. It is not the scientists. It is the church of Jesus Christ. We alone have the knowledge and the weapons at our disposal to deal with the satanic principalities and powers in the heavenlies that seek to dominate the course of human history.

In the second part of Ezekiel 28, the prophet turns his attention to the king of Tyre. As we read these words, we will see very clearly that this could not be a description of a human being. The Lord instructs Ezekiel to speak the following:

> Son of man, take up a lamentation for the king of Tyre, and say to him, "Thus says the Lord GOD: 'You were the seal of perfection, full of wisdom and perfect in beauty. You were in Eden, the garden of God; every precious stone was your covering: the sardius, topaz, and diamond, beryl, onyx, and jasper, sapphire, turquoise, and emerald with gold.

The workmanship of your timbrels and pipes was prepared for you on the day you were created.'"   (Ezekiel 28:12–13)

Notice that this king of Tyre is an angelic being, yet he is a *created* being. There is only one Person who is uncreated, and that is God. All the rest of us are created. There is a false belief today, which has even infiltrated the church, that claims we can somehow become gods. Let me just state, my dear friend, that this is ridiculous. The created can never become the uncreated. The passage in Ezekiel 28 continues with verse 14:

You were the anointed cherub who covers [covers the throne of God]; *I established you; you were on the holy mountain of God; you walked back and forth in the midst of fiery stones.*

Again, it is obviously not a human who is being addressed.

You were perfect in your ways from the day you were created, till iniquity [or rebellion] *was found in you.*   (verse 15)

Who is the king of Tyre? Lucifer. His fall is described in verse 17:

Your heart was lifted up because of your beauty; you corrupted your wisdom for the sake of your splendor; I cast you to the ground, I laid you before kings, that they might gaze at you.

WHY LUCIFER FELL

What was the reason for Lucifer's fall? What was his sin? *"Your heart was lifted up."* It was pride. Pride is the original sin. Theologically speaking, we use the term "original sin" to refer to the sin nature that human beings inherited from Adam after his own rebellion and fall. However, that is not really a correct use of the term. The "original sin" is pride. In my opinion, pride is the root of every other sin. And Satan's main tactic against human beings, in order to get us to reject God, is to stir up in us a condition of pride. I once heard a fellow preacher say, "Pride is the only sin of which Satan never makes you feel guilty." There is a lot of truth in that.

Learning where pride came from is just the beginning. Our next task is to figure out what we can do about it.

12

THE ONLY REMEDY

Now that we have acknowledged the universal problem of pride, we must raise the question, "How can we handle this issue?" God is absolutely straightforward and specific about how to deal with it.

GOD RESISTS THE PROUD

To find out what the Lord has to say about pride, we will begin by looking at a passage in 1 Peter that quotes from the Old Testament book of Proverbs:

God resists the proud, but gives grace to the humble.   (1 Peter 5:5)

The original verse from Proverbs is an even stronger statement about God's response to pride:

Surely He scorns the scornful, but gives grace to the humble.
(Proverbs 3:34)

Do you see how futile it is to pray to God out of pride? If you do so, God will resist you. He will stand against you. You may use the finest words and cite the most eloquent Scriptures. But if you are praying out of pride, God will resist you, and your prayers will not accomplish what you hope they will.

Next, we come to 1 Peter 1:6, which begins with the word *"therefore."* In my teachings, I have often pointed out that when you find a "therefore" in the Scriptures, you want to find out what it is "there for"! This *"therefore"* connects to the previous verse:

> *Therefore* [because *"God resists the proud, but gives grace to the humble"*] *humble yourselves under the mighty hand of God, that He may exalt you in due time.*   (1 Peter 5:6)

The only remedy for pride is to humble ourselves. In that regard, we need to take note of one fact: the Scriptures are clear that you cannot ask God to make you humble. The Lord always says, "Humble yourself." God can humiliate you (and He may have to do that at times to correct you or get your attention), but only you can make yourself humble. How is that possible? You can only do it when the Holy Spirit moves upon you. You cannot do it in your own strength. But when the Holy Spirit touches your heart, you will find the ability to humble yourself.

THE RESPONSE OF HUMILITY

As an example of humility, I think of the sinful woman who stood behind Jesus, weeping and washing His feet with her tears. (See Luke 7:36–50.) The background to this event is that Jesus had been invited, among other guests, to have a meal at the home of a particular Pharisee, a religious ruler. Yet this woman, who is never named, was the only one who walked out of that gathering in a freed condition. Why? What did she do? She humbled herself. She could not have done more than she did. She washed Jesus's feet with her tears and dried them with her hair. Then, she anointed His feet with perfume. Such humility is the only remedy for pride.

People often use the adage "Pride goes before a fall," thinking they are quoting from the Bible. But that is not what the Bible actually says. It says, *"Pride goes before destruction, and a haughty spirit before a fall"* (Proverbs 16:18). If you tolerate pride in your life and do not deal with it in the scriptural way, it will ultimately destroy you. Sadly, it may well destroy your family too.

Let me reemphasize that God will not do the humbling for us. He will give us the grace to do it. He will send the Holy Spirit to help us, and the Holy Spirit will entreat us to humble ourselves. But we have to make the response. We have to humble ourselves.

WHAT IS TRUE HUMILITY?

Please understand that humility is not an emotion. So, don't try to "feel" humble. Frankly, that is ridiculous. *Humility is a decision of the will expressed in action*, such as the action of the woman who washed Jesus's feet with her tears.

In His teachings, Jesus gave some vivid illustrations of true humility. Let's look at one of them from Luke 14, where Jesus was at a banquet given by another Pharisee.

> *He told a parable to those who were invited, when he noted how they chose the best places.* (Luke 14:7)

Everybody at the dinner went for the top seats. They came in and went straight for the head table because that is where they wanted to be—and to be seen. But Jesus told them:

> *When you are invited by anyone to a wedding feast, do not sit down in the best place, lest one more honorable than you be invited by him; and he who invited you and him come and say to you, "Give place to this man," and then you begin with shame to take the lowest place.*
> (verses 8–9)

Jesus is so practical! He was saying, "Start by taking the lowest place, because then you can't go any lower." There is a short poem along these lines by John Bunyan, the author of *Pilgrim's Progress*, that greatly appeals to me:

He that is down needs fear no fall,
He that is low no pride;
He that is humble ever shall
Have God to be his guide.

What is the one safe place to be? It is on your face before God. Often, when Ruth and I were invited to teach at a conference, before the first session, we would get on the floor on our faces before God. We knew how dangerous it would be to minister spiritual truths without having met the conditions for them ourselves—especially on the subject of pride. So, we would humble ourselves before the Lord. My words to Him were that I had nothing to offer apart from what He gave me, saying, "Lord, I have nothing to give to these people except what comes from Your heart, through my heart, to them."

Jesus continued His banquet parable with this advice:

But when you are invited, go and sit down in the lowest place, so that when he who invited you comes he may say to you, "Friend, go up higher." Then you will have glory in the presence of those who sit at the table with you. (Luke 14:10)

Do you see how practical Jesus is? Do you see how simple He makes it? Humility is not an emotion. It is not a hyper-spiritual display. It is a decision that is expressed by the way you act. Do you go for the top place or do you take the lowest place? You may *talk* about being humble. But if you always aim for the highest place, it is all talk and no substance.

A UNIVERSAL LAW OF HUMILITY

Then, Jesus gave us a universal law. When I say "a universal law," I mean a law that governs the universe—not just human life or life on this earth, but all of life.

For whoever exalts himself will be humbled, and he who humbles himself will be exalted. (Luke 14:11)

There are no exceptions to this law. It applies to each of us. Do you want to be exalted? Then humble yourself. But if you exalt yourself, you will be humbled. In other words, as I see it, *you determine how high you end up by how low you start.*

13

SEVEN STEPS

We continue to explore, in practical ways, what it means to humble ourselves before God. We have noted that the lower you go, the higher you will finish. This result is not an accident. It is not an experiment. It is a law that governs the entire universe.

JESUS'S HUMILITY AND EXALTATION

Most of us are confronted by embarrassing situations at times. Other people may insult or humiliate us. They may treat us with contempt or reject us. My dear friend, whenever this happens, rejoice—because you have been given a wonderful opportunity to humble yourself.

The law of humility is most wonderfully illustrated in the life of Jesus, particularly as described by Paul in Philippians 2:5–11. This passage reminds me of the amazing contrast between Jesus and Lucifer. Lucifer was an archangel with access to the throne of God. However, instead of being content with that place, he sought the highest place—and fell to the depths. Jesus, by His divine nature, was already equal with God. But He humbled Himself to the lowest place to redeem human beings to their heavenly Father. Therefore, God has exalted Him to the highest place.

It is a remarkable fact that the epistle to the Philippians was written by Paul when he was in prison. Who knows what writing materials he had available to him? He probably didn't even have a desk to work from. Yet the literary construction of what he writes is absolutely perfect! The more you analyze it, the more perfect you see it is. Presenting first the humility of Jesus and then His exaltation, Paul describes seven downward steps Jesus took, and then seven steps whereby God raised Him up. I will comment more on this structure later in the chapter. Let us look at the entire passage, and then we will consider its individual statements:

> *Let this mind be in you which was also in Christ Jesus, who, being in the form of God, did not consider it robbery to be equal with God, but made Himself of no reputation, taking the form of a bondservant, and coming in the likeness of men. And being found in appearance as a man, he humbled Himself and became obedient to the point of death, even the death of the cross. Therefore God also has highly exalted Him and given Him the name which is above every name, that at the name of Jesus every knee should bow, of those in heaven, and of those on earth, and of those under the earth, and that every tongue should confess that Jesus Christ is Lord, to the glory of God the Father.*
>
> (Philippians 2:5–11)

To begin, Paul writes, *"Let this mind be in you which was also in Christ Jesus..."* (Philippians 2:5). In other words, we must learn to think the way Jesus thought.

Then Paul describes how Jesus humbled Himself: *"...who, being in the form of God, did not consider it robbery to be equal with God"* (verse 6). I have seen this translated as, "...did not consider equality with God something He had to snatch because He had it by divine right." Jesus didn't have to grab for equality with God. It was already His. Do you see the remarkable difference? Lucifer reached up and grabbed—and fell. Jesus lowered Himself—and God raised Him up.

SEVEN STEPS OF HUMILITY

Now we come to the first of the seven downward steps Jesus took: He *"made Himself of no reputation"* (Philippians 2:7). The original Greek says

He "emptied Himself." Charles Wesley wrote a line about this in one of his hymns: "He emptied Himself of all but love."[3]

Therefore, this is step one: *"made Himself of no reputation,"* or "emptied Himself."

Step two: *"taking the form of a bondservant"* (verse 7). Jesus could have been a servant at the level of an angel, but He continued downward.

Step three: *"coming in the likeness of men"* (verse 7). He came down to the level of humanity. However, He didn't come down to the level of human perfection Adam enjoyed before the fall. Though Jesus was completely sinless, He came all the way down to the level of the men and women of His age.

Step four: *"found in appearance as a man"* (verse 8). When the people of Jesus's day looked at Him, there was nothing in His outward appearance that indicated His divine nature.

Step five: *"humbled Himself..."* (verse 8). He was a humble man. He was not a prince or a priest. He was a carpenter. There is no reproach in being a carpenter, but it certainly was not the highest level of society in His day.

Step six: *"became obedient to the point of death"* (verse 8). He lived as a man, and He died as a man.

Step seven, the ultimate step down: *"even the death of the cross"* (verse 8). Crucifixion was the form of death used for criminals. It was the utmost extreme of shame and agony.

These seven downward steps are our pattern. *"Let this mind be in you which was also in Christ Jesus"* (verse 5). We must learn to think the way Jesus thought and act the way Jesus acted. Don't reach up. Don't grab. Instead, stoop down. See how you can humble yourself and go lower.

SEVEN STEPS OF EXALTATION

Next, let's look at the seven steps of exaltation that follow the seven steps of humility. Please notice that in Philippians 2:9, there is another instance of a *"therefore,"* indicating the effect of something that came before.

---

3. "And Can It Be That I Should Gain," 1738.

This exaltation was a result of Jesus humbling Himself. I want to emphasize that Jesus was not exalted because He was a favorite Son. He was exalted because He met the conditions to be exalted. He is our pattern.

Step one: *"Therefore God has also highly exalted Him"* (verse 9).

Step two: *"and given Him the name which is above every name"* (verse 9).

Step three: *"that at the name of Jesus every knee should bow"* (verse 10).

Step four: *"of those in heaven"* (verse 10).

Step five: *"of those on earth"* (verse 10).

Step six: *"of those under the earth"* (verse 10).

And step seven: *"that every tongue should confess that Jesus Christ is Lord, to the glory of God the Father"* (verse 11).

I mentioned earlier that I was a logician and an analyst of words before I became a preacher. Consequently, I delight in the perfect structure of this passage in Philippians: seven steps down and seven steps up, joined by the word *"therefore."* This *"therefore,"* my dear reader, applies to the life of every one of us! The measure to which we go down will determine the measure to which God raises us up.

I once published a series of messages entitled "The Way Up Is Down." That is how life in God truly works. Nonetheless, I don't think people felt attracted to that series of messages—they were never very popular. But the message is true: *the way up is down!*

Thus, if we want God to hear our prayers for revival, we cannot bypass the first condition: *"If My people...will humble themselves"* (2 Chronicles 7:14). If we will not humble ourselves, everything else is in vain. You can pray as much as you like; you can fast; you can cry out to God; you can preach. But God says the first condition is to "humble yourself." And He means it. *"God resists the proud, but gives grace to the humble"* (1 Peter 5:5).

14

A LESSON IN HUMILITY

The question we are investigating is "How can we humble ourselves?" Whenever possible, I like to give a practical application of what I am teaching. To illustrate the process of humbling oneself, I will draw from one of my own personal experiences—one that was particularly painful. Somebody once said, "The school of experience is the best school in the world, but it's also the most expensive." I would add, "And the most painful!"

GOD'S FAITHFULNESS

At the end of 1990 and the beginning of 1991, Ruth and I took a six-month sabbatical to get away from everything, to seek God, and—we imagined—to relax and rest. We went to a beautiful part of the world: Hawaii. There we stayed in a condominium that looked right out over the Pacific, and we thought, "Now we are going to have a wonderful time of Bible study and fellowship, and everything is going to be lovely." However, it was exactly the opposite! We never experienced six more painful months in our entire lives. Did everything go wrong? No, everything went God's way—not our way.

Looking back, I can honestly thank God for those six months. But our time in Hawaii was full of bewildering challenges. During this period, I became desperately ill with a heart condition that is very difficult to diagnose and cannot be cured without antibiotics. It is called subacute bacterial endocarditis (SBE), which is an inflammation of the lining of the heart. I had been suffering from it progressively for several months before it was diagnosed.

God had ordained for us to take the sabbatical, and later, a dear friend said to us, "I think that sabbatical saved your life, because if you had been traveling around as you usually do, you would not have had time to stop and go to the doctor and be thoroughly examined. It would have killed you." This was a testimony to the faithfulness of God.

So there I was with this illness. I believed in divine healing, and I had preached on divine healing. I had prayed for the sick and seen them recover. Yet, I myself was now sick. My problem was not emotional. I was not afraid of death. My problem was intellectual. I thought, "What has gone wrong? Why doesn't it work?" Let me say, *never* ask the question, "Why doesn't 'it' work?" "It" is not an "it." "It" is a *He*. The question becomes very different when you put *He* in place of *it*: "Why doesn't He [God] work?"

AN INTERVIEW WITH JESUS

God has always had a habit of speaking to me at about two o'clock in the morning. Sometimes, if I am wide awake at two, I am pretty sure God has something He wants to communicate to me. I don't want to use the phrase "God spoke to me" in an offhand way. As I mentioned, I once heard God speak audibly, and I have heard God's messages communicated through the gifts of the Spirit, such as a word of knowledge. But many times, when He speaks, it is simply an inward impression.

One night, as I lay in bed in Hawaii, I had no idea I was going to end up in the hospital for almost three weeks. But at two in the morning, I was saying to God in my heart, "What has gone wrong?"

I then had an "interview" with Jesus, which reminded me of Paul's statement about how we will one day stand before the judgment seat of Christ:

For we must all appear before the judgment seat of Christ, that each one may receive the things done in the body, according to what he has done, whether good or bad. (2 Corinthians 5:10)

This judgment by Christ will not be one of condemnation, but rather a judgment of believers to assess their faithfulness and bestow eternal rewards. In my interview with Jesus, it was as if He was very calmly—I would even say unemotionally—without ever being condemnatory, opening up my understanding to see many different ways in which I had failed to live the way I should have.

I had never been involved in adultery, drunkenness, or misappropriation of funds—the snares into which many preachers fall. By the grace of God, those were not my problems. I was a faithful, effective preacher, involved in meetings and conferences. What the Lord wanted to show me, however, was how "carnal" I had often been. *Carnal* is a biblical term for living according to the fallen, sinful nature. It is also called "living in the flesh"—rather than living in the Spirit. (We will examine the meaning of "the flesh" in chapter 17 of this book.) To me, to be carnal is to live as if there isn't any eternity. Any time we lose sight of the fact that eternity is our true destination, and that we are here on earth only briefly, for relatively few years, we are being carnal.

The Word of God says, *"He who sows to his flesh will of the flesh reap corruption"* (Galatians 6:8). What is sickness? It is a form of corruption. My meeting with Jesus at two in the morning totally cleared my mind. I now had the answer to my earlier question, "Why doesn't He work?" I realized there was nothing wrong with God—He had not failed me. I had been carnal.

UNDER CONVICTION

But that was not all. God also showed me there were sins in my life I had not confessed. At least one of them went back almost forty years. It wasn't a terrible sin—it was more of an embarrassing sin because it was so stupid! But God made clear to me what I had to do. From what the Scriptures say, I knew that if we want our sins forgiven, there is a step we have to take. We have to confess them: *"If we confess our sins, He is faithful and just to forgive us our sins and to cleanse us from all unrighteousness"* (1 John 1:9).

As I expressed earlier, I personally believe we cannot claim forgiveness for sins we have not confessed. One of the great, faithful ministries of the Holy Spirit is to convict us of sin. This is not to condemn us, but to liberate us—because when you are under conviction, you can confess your sins and be set free.

Hours after my interview with Jesus, I was admitted to the hospital and ended up staying for nineteen days. I was treated very kindly. For some preachers, because of their belief in divine healing, I think they tend to speak in an ungracious way about doctors, nurses, and hospitals. In the past, I have at times done the same myself. I want to repent of that. I thank God for the doctors and nurses at that hospital and the care I received there.

I want to mention something else I thank God for (and this isn't a "super-spiritual" statement): I thank God for antibiotics! I was on intravenous antibiotics for six weeks, and this treatment saved my life.

CHASTENED

There was something else God gave me in connection with this experience. It is described in Psalm 118:13–18, where the psalmist is addressing his enemy the devil. The passage begins in this way:

You pushed me violently, that I might fall. (verse 13)

The devil undoubtedly did the same in my situation. He pushed me violently to make me fall. However, as the writer says:

But the LORD helped me. The LORD is my strength and song, and He has become my salvation. (Psalm 118:13–14)

The psalm continues:

The voice of rejoicing and salvation is in the tents of the righteous; the right hand of the LORD does valiantly. The right hand of the LORD is exalted; the right hand of the LORD does valiantly. (verses 15–16)

This is the portion of the psalm I particularly want to emphasize:

I shall not die, but live, and declare the works of the LORD. *The* LORD
has chastened me severely, but He has not given me over to death.

(verses 17–18)

My dear reader, if God doesn't give you over to death, you will not die. He certainly chastened me severely, but that chastening was a gift to me. He brought me face-to-face with aspects of my life, character, and ministry that were displeasing to Him. He had blessed my ministry for many years. But it is a mistake to assume that if God blesses you, it means He approves of everything you do.

I am grateful for everything the Lord revealed to me during that six-month ordeal in Hawaii. Most of all, I am grateful for His chastening. It changed my outlook forever on an important biblical principle that is inseparably tied to self-humbling. This will be the focus of our next chapter.

15

THE GIFT OF CONFESSION

During my illness in Hawaii, God showed me there were many areas in my life about which I needed to repent, confess, and seek forgiveness. I shared the story of how the Lord took me through this process of chastening. I shared the key to self-humbling, which is not complicated: it is the confession of our sins.

TAKING RESPONSIBILITY

You cannot stay proud in the presence of God while you are confessing your humiliating, embarrassing, and personal sins. We need to call them by the right name. We are confessing "sins"—not "problems." Many people don't want to use the word *sin* today. They want to call their wrongdoings *problems*. However, the blood of Jesus does not cleanse us from problems. The blood of Jesus only cleanses us from one thing: sin. (See, for example, 1 John 1:7.)

If we don't confess our sin, God won't cleanse us from it. We are answerable to Him for that sin, and we have to take responsibility for what we have done. We can't blame our parents, our spouse, our pastor, or anyone else. If we have sinned, there is only one remedy: confess it to the Lord.

A REMEDY FOR SIN

If we confess our sins, [God] is faithful and just to forgive us our sins and to cleanse us from all unrighteousness. (1 John 1:9)

Do you really believe this verse? No words can express how important it is in our lives. *There is a remedy for sin.* I have lived in communities and cultures where people did not know there was a remedy for sin. How privileged we are that God has revealed this to us! I love the old hymn that says,

> There is a fountain filled with blood
> Drawn from Immanuel's veins;
> And sinners, plunged beneath that flood,
> Lose all their guilty stains.[4]

I thank God for the blood of Jesus. Nothing will cleanse us and purify our hearts except for the precious blood of the Lamb of God, the Lord Jesus Christ. He shed His blood so that we might be forgiven, cleansed, and justified.

UNDERSTANDING JUSTIFICATION

Do you know what the word *justified* means for the believer? It means, "I am 'just as if I'd' never sinned," made righteous with the righteousness of Jesus through His blood. It is not our righteousness, but His. And His righteousness is a righteousness that has never known sin. For the Christian, to be justified is a glorious reality!

Justification is not a complicated theological formula. Here is a simple illustration of what *justified* means: It is as if I am being tried for a crime for which the mandatory penalty is death, and I know I am guilty. But when the judge gives his verdict, he says, "Not guilty!" Now, at such a moment, if my spouse were sitting beside me, would I simply turn to her and say, "That is so nice, isn't it, dear?" No! I would throw my arms around her neck and say, "Sweetheart, I'm free!"

4. William Cowper, "There Is a Fountain Filled with Blood," 1772, *Hymns for the Living Church* (Carol Stream, IL: Hope Publishing Company, 1974).

If Christians could truly understand the depth of the degree of pardon they have received through Jesus Christ, they would get really excited! When I was growing up in the Anglican Church, I loved the praises of the Anglican liturgy. But as a twelve-year old boy, I would look at the people walking out of church after the service and say to myself, "I don't think they really believe what they said." Those words were so glorious I couldn't understand why they didn't get excited. In fact, it is almost a sin not to get excited about the pardon we receive when we are justified.

THE HEAVY BURDEN OF SIN

King David was a man after God's own heart (see 1 Samuel 13:14; Acts 13:22), and he did a lot of confessing of sin. I don't know whether you have ever noticed in the Scriptures how much confessing he did. Something else to note is how many times he struggled with sickness. In Psalm 38, David says:

> *There is no soundness in my flesh because of Your anger, nor any health in my bones because of my sin.* (verse 3)

If you are seeking healing, check to see whether your sickness may be due to sin. Sometimes that can be one of the contributing factors. We know that David was a man after God's heart. God loved him and he loved God. However, he admits, *"Nor is there any health in my bones because of my sin."* In the next verse, David says,

> *For my iniquities have gone over my head; like a heavy burden they are too heavy for me.* (Psalm 38:4)

If we allow unconfessed sin to pile up in our lives, it can become burden added upon burden that soon is higher than our heads. Are you staggering through life under the burden of unconfessed sin? If it could happen to David, it could happen to any of us. I think that is a problem with much of the church. We are staggering under a burden of unconfessed sin. It could be part of the reason for the lack of real joy, real life, freedom to witness, and concern for the unsaved that is found in the modern church. And every sin we commit without confessing adds to that burden.

SELF-HUMBLING

Confessing our sins to God is what I call "vertical self-humbling"—we humble ourselves in our vertical relationship to God. Confessing our sins to other people whom we have wronged or offended is "horizontal self-humbling." The latter might be the most challenging. For example, many husbands have been proud, arrogant, and insensitive in their relationships with their wives. What do they need to do? They need to humble themselves before their wives and confess their failings.

Wives may also need to do the same, but I believe this is a particular problem for husbands. One of the hardest pills for a husband to swallow is to humble himself before his wife and apologize to her. If you are a husband, how long has it been since you said anything like the following to your wife? "I'm sorry I got angry." "I'm sorry I was so insensitive." "I'm sorry I didn't consider your feelings." "I'm sorry I was rude." "I'm sorry I ignored you when you were trying to talk to me." If a husband were to confess such things to his wife sincerely, it would change the atmosphere in his home in a miraculous way.

Ruth and I came to a place where we would regularly confess our sins to one another. This is a scriptural practice. James 5:16 says,

> *Confess your trespasses* [sins] *to one another, and pray for one another, that you may be healed.*

This is horizontal self-humbling. You may have to go to your pastor and say, "I have to confess I've said critical things about you to other people." Or, if you are a pastor, you might have to go to a member of your congregation and say, "I haven't treated you with the love and concern I should have given you." There is no class of persons who is exempt from the requirement of confession of sin. Not only is confession the right step to take, but it is also a key for physical healing. "*Confess your* [sins] *to one another, and pray for one another, that you may be healed.*" In other words, unconfessed sin is a barrier to healing.

CONFESSING OUR SINS

In the 1950s, I read the journals of John Wesley and was deeply impacted by them. I was a Pentecostal, and I thought the Pentecostals had everything. But when I read Wesley's journals, I had to admit, "He has a lot of insights we Pentecostals don't have."

Somewhere in his journals, he describes the origin of one of the strongest Methodist societies of his day. I believe it was in Yorkshire. It started with ten people who agreed to meet together every week and confess their faults to one another. How many people in churches do that today?

You see, you can't build a church on a wrong foundation. A church is built with people who are in healthy, right relationships. The same applies to the family. A home is built out of relationships. If you are a parent, have you ever asked your children for forgiveness after being thoughtless toward them or wronging them?

Many years ago, I became unreasonably angry with one of my daughters and said things to her I never should have said. Afterward, I had a strange feeling of pressure in my chest, and I thought, "Where is this coming from?" Then I read Ecclesiastes 7:9, *"Do not hasten in your spirit to be angry, for anger rests in the bosom of fools."* I knew then what my problem was. I also knew there was only one solution, but it wouldn't be easy to follow through with it. I had to go to my daughter and say, "I'm sorry I became angry with you. I shouldn't have spoken to you like that." When I did, the pressure immediately lifted from my chest.

Thus, I believe the key to self-humbling is confession of sin. At least, it is a good place to start. We are to confess our sins to God, and confess them to one another.

THE HEART IS DECEITFUL

How can we know what to confess? Here is my advice: As I mentioned earlier, in chapter 6, when dealing with unconfessed sin, don't start to probe into your own character, because the deeper you go, the worse it will become. That is not God's remedy. God's remedy comes through the Holy Spirit. The Spirit convicts us of sin, of righteousness, and of judgment. (See John 16:8.) So, allow the Holy Spirit to convict you of what you need to confess.

Let me explain this idea further by pointing out two verses about the heart from Jeremiah 17, beginning with verse 9:

The heart is deceitful above all things, and desperately wicked; who can know it? (Jeremiah 17:9)

In 1947, I was attending The Hebrew University in Jerusalem as a guest student. I was listening to a lecture by the professor of Hebrew language, and he commented on the above verse. This man was not a believer, either as a Jew or in relation to any other religion. However, his comment was that the Hebrew word translated here as *"deceitful"* is *akov*, which is the same word used in the name *Ja-akov*, or Jacob, which means "supplanter." Then, he pointed out that because of the way the word is formed, it is not passive but active. It is not that the heart is deceived, but rather that the heart is deceitful. In other words, *the heart deceives.* This professor had no spiritual intentions in mind, but I thought to myself, "I have just learned one of the most valuable lessons of my life. My heart is deceitful. It doesn't tell me the truth. It deceives me. I cannot rely on my heart to tell me its true condition."

OUR TRUE CONDITION

The next verse in Jeremiah 17 says this,

I, the LORD, *search the heart, I test the mind, even to give every man according to his ways, according to the fruit of his doings.* (verse 10)

There is only one Person who truly knows what is in your heart—and it is not you! It is the Lord. If you ask Him, He will very gently and graciously begin to unfold to you the true condition of your heart. The great preacher Charles G. Finney reportedly said, "I am convinced that if a sinner could truly see the nature of his own heart and how evil it is, he could not survive the sight." We have a very dim concept of how deceitful and evil our own heart is. Once again, the only One who can show us the true nature of our heart is the Lord, through the Holy Spirit.

In Matthew 12:28, Jesus says, *"If I cast out demons by the Spirit of God...."* In Luke 11:20, He says, *"If I cast out demons with the finger of God."* This tells us that the Holy Spirit is God's "finger." When God deals with you, He doesn't put His whole hand on your heart and say, "There is some problem here." He puts His finger on a particular area of your life and says, "This is where the problem is." He will be very specific in naming your problem, as unwelcome as that information might be.

Therefore, do not rely on your own heart to tell you the truth about yourself. The only One who is qualified to do that is the Lord. He will be very gracious. He won't shock you with everything all at once. He knows you would not be able to stand it.

Years ago, my first wife and I had a Christian maid of Arabic descent. She became our maid while we were living in Ramallah, in what was then Palestine, and later, she moved with us to England and lived in our home. She never learned to read, so she couldn't read the Bible. Her life was, I would say, somewhat inconsistent. There were times when she was infuriating, and there were other times when she was wonderful. But she got by, and the way she got by in her Christian life was that when God convicted her of sin, she really poured out her heart to Him in repentance. I can remember to this day some of the prayers she prayed in Arabic. She knew how to humble herself. What a precious gift to know how to humble yourself before Almighty God.

THE PRAYER OF DAVID

When you think about King David and the sins he committed (including adultery and murder), it is truly amazing he was called a man after God's own heart. So don't be surprised or discouraged, my dear friend, when God puts His finger on sinful areas in your life that you weren't even aware you needed to repent of, confess, and receive forgiveness for. You can still be a man or woman after God's own heart if you learn to humble yourself before Him.

As noted earlier in this chapter, I believe there is a great cloud of unconfessed sin over the church of Jesus Christ. I don't say that to condemn us, because God is not out to condemn us. He wants to forgive and liberate us, if we will only confess our sins.

How can we know what God requires us to confess? Again, we need to ask God to show us through His Holy Spirit. The prayer of David in Psalm 139:23–24 is this type of appeal:

Search me, O God, and know my heart; try me, and know my anxiet-
ies [or my anxious thoughts, or my worries]; *and see if there is any*
wicked way in me, and lead me in the way everlasting.

As we close this chapter and part three of this book, I want to challenge you to consider praying this prayer of David in relation to yourself.
When we pray a prayer like this, I believe it demands that we spend time
alone in God's presence to hear His answer. Let us open our hearts to God
now by praying the following prayer together:

"*Search me, O God, and know my heart; try me, and know my*
[anxious thoughts]; *and see if there is any wicked way in me, and*
lead me in the way everlasting." Lord God, show me the things
in my life that are not pleasing to You. Show me the ways I've
offended other people. Show me the ways in which I may have
hurt my own family. Lord, please deal with me gently. Don't
take me too fast. I really want to get sin out of my life. I truly
desire to humble myself. Thank You for leading me in the way
everlasting. In the name of Jesus, amen.

Now that you and I have lifted up this prayer, we must be prepared for
God to take us seriously. If we say to Him, "*Search me, O God,*" as David
did, He is going to search us. You and I can expect Him to show us those
areas in our lives we need to confess. Let us confess them. Let us repent, receive God's forgiveness, and ask for the power of the Holy Spirit to change
us.

PART FOUR:

ELIMINATING LEGALISM

16

A BIG PROBLEM

Would you agree that the current course of your nation—and other nations of the world—needs to be changed? I believe that when our lives are aligned with the purposes of God, the Holy Spirit will stir within our hearts—and He will begin to flow like a fountain out of our lives and into the world around us. Out of those small beginnings, God can do a work that will affect the destiny of nations.

God has not asked us to sit back and wait for Him to bring about a revival. He prefers to work with us. He is waiting for us to open our hearts to Him and align ourselves with His will. In order to do this, it is necessary for us to apply the seven principles of revival we are exploring in this book. As we apply these foundational principles, we can become the people God desires us to be, and He can bring revival.

To review what we have covered so far, in parts one and two, we learned that the first two conditions we must meet are loving others and loving God. In essence, we must fulfill the "law of love," which Jesus summarized in this way: to love the Lord our God with all our heart, mind, and soul, and to love our neighbor as ourselves. Regarding our obligation to love God fully, we saw from the parable of the rich young ruler that Jesus asks us to relinquish any possession or person more important to us than He is—including our own lives.

In part three, we addressed the first of three obstacles to revival—the universal problem of pride. We saw that the process of humbling ourselves involves repentance and confession. God calls upon us to humble ourselves before Him.

In all of these steps, we have an active role. For this reason, we must remember that any prediction suggesting that revival will come simply of its own accord, without our involvement, is deceptive. We have a vital part to play in revival.

THE SNARE OF LEGALISM

Let us begin part four of our study with this question: What do you consider to be the greatest problem that has troubled the church of Jesus Christ from the first century until now? Would you say it is the devil? Lack of unity? Worldliness? Deception? Spiritual warfare? My own answer to this question might come as a surprise to you. But it is my considered opinion that the greatest single hindrance to the purposes of God in the church is *legalism*.

What is legalism? It is trying to obtain God's favor by what we do, or trying to attain salvation by earning it. The majority of professing Christians around the world today are caught in some form of this snare of legalism.

I am also aware that the opposite problem exists in some sectors of Christianity—what is called *antinomianism* ("against law"). This involves a refusal to accept *any* law and an insistence upon going one's own way. That path, of course, is totally contrary to Scripture. According to my personal observations, in many cases, antinomianism can be a reaction against legalism. The damaging effects of legalism can prompt people to turn to an antinomian viewpoint. In this way, both are expressions of legalism.

THE CRUX OF THE MATTER

In chapter 2 of this book, we examined one of the most important questions ever asked—one that is also central to our discussion here. It is found in Job 9:2:

How can a man be righteous before God?

That is a key question. How can someone be righteous before God? As noted earlier, Job's three friends ridiculed the idea that anybody could be righteous before God. They argued that God is so completely holy, and we are so unholy and unworthy, that it is ridiculous to suppose anybody could be righteous before Him. However, we find God's own answer to Job's question in the writings of Paul in the book of Romans:

> For I am not ashamed of the gospel of Christ, for it is the power of God to salvation for everyone who believes, for the Jew first and also for the Greek. For in it the righteousness of God is revealed from faith to faith; as it is written, "The just shall live by faith."   (Romans 1:16–17)

What is revealed in the gospel? "*The righteousness of God.*" The key word here, which occurs three times, is "*faith.*" Righteousness is achieved only through faith; there is no other way to achieve righteousness.

In the third chapter of Philippians, the apostle shares a little of his personal background as a very zealous Orthodox Jew. Paul had observed everything in the law that he could observe, and yet he declares:

> But what things were gain to me, these I have counted loss for Christ. Yet indeed I also count all things loss for the excellence of the knowledge of Christ Jesus my Lord, for whom I have suffered the loss of all things, and count them as rubbish, that I may gain Christ and be found in Him, not having my own righteousness, which is from the law, but that which is through faith in Christ, the righteousness which is from God by faith.   (Philippians 3:7–9)

This is the crux of the matter. Paul is saying that it is not about his own righteousness, achieved by keeping a set of rules (legalism), but rather about the righteousness that comes from God by faith.

DESTINATION: RESURRECTION

Paul then speaks about the outcome of this righteousness:

That I may know Him [Jesus] *and the power of His resurrection, and the fellowship of His sufferings, being conformed to His death, if, by any means, I may attain to the resurrection from the dead.*

(Philippians 3:10–11)

In this passage, when Paul speaks about "attaining to the resurrection," he is not talking about the final resurrection. In the original Greek, the word translated *"resurrection"* in Philippians 3:11 literally means "out resurrection," referring to the first resurrection only for the righteous. (See Revelation 20:5.)

Why is this important? Many believers have the idea that the aim of the Christian life is to get to heaven. However, did you know that getting to heaven is *not* the true aim of the Christian life? Heaven is a wonderful stopping-off place, but it is not the destination! The final destination is the resurrection! God will create a new earth in which He dwells directly with His people. (See Revelation 21:1–3.) That is when God's purposes will be complete.

You see, when we die, while our spirits are in heaven, our bodies will be decomposing in the grave. But Jesus died to redeem spirit, soul, *and* body. Redemption is not complete until the body has been redeemed along with the spirit and the soul. This will occur at the first resurrection—the "out resurrection"—when the dead in Christ will be raised, and *"we shall all be changed—in a moment, in the twinkling of an eye…. For this corruptible must put on incorruption, and this mortal must put on immortality"* (1 Corinthians 15:51–53). That is where I am headed—and that is where Paul set his sights. No matter what it would cost him, Paul did not want to miss this resurrection.

FAITH IS A GIFT

I don't believe anyone will accidentally drift into the first resurrection. I think attaining this resurrection requires a sense of purpose, a set of the will, and a commitment to live a certain way. But coming into the resurrection is not possible for any of us by the religion of works. The religion of works will never get us there. It is only by *the righteousness which is from God by faith*" (Philippians 3:9).

The alternative to righteousness through faith is legalism. Let's review the meaning of *legalism*: it is seeking to obtain righteousness by what you do—by the laws you keep, the rules you observe, the good deeds you do.

Our churches today are full of people who *think* they are attaining righteousness with God by leading a good life, by keeping the Ten Commandments, by obeying the Golden Rule, and so forth. However, good conduct and following various rules do not bring the righteousness of God. There is only one way to attain righteousness. It is very simple: by believing in Jesus Christ.

As we just read in Romans 1:16, *"The gospel of Christ…is the power of God to salvation for everyone who **believes**."* And Ephesians 2:8 says, *"For by grace you have been saved **through faith** [and lest we begin to get conceited], and that not of yourselves; it is the gift of God."* Faith is a gift. In other words, we didn't have the faith to be saved until God gave us the faith to be saved.

This truth was so clear to me in my own experience. When I was first confronted with the gospel, I really wanted to believe, but I wasn't able to until God gave me the faith. It was a gift. It came miraculously, supernaturally. The moment He gave me the faith, I believed. People's faith can be blocked by various obstacles. Before coming to Christ, I had been deep into the practice of yoga. My involvement in it was the big obstacle between Jesus and me. I could believe that Jesus was a wonderful guru, or a wonderful teacher, but I could not believe He was the Son of God. Yet the moment I was released from the spirit of yoga, I knew instantly that Jesus was the Son of God.

UPSET OVER LEGALISM

One of Paul's epistles in the New Testament deals specifically with legalism: Galatians. We see this clearly from the way Paul begins his letter to the Galatian believers. In most of his epistles, Paul starts by thanking

God for the grace of God in the lives of the people to whom he is writing, even if those believers have been making a lot of mistakes. For example, in 1 Corinthians, Paul addresses some serious problems in the Corinthian church. There was a man who was living with his father's wife. There were people who were getting drunk at the Lord's Table. There was a certain amount of quarreling, division, and selfishness among them. But in spite of all those problems, Paul addresses them with these words:

> *I thank my God always concerning you for the grace of God which was given to you by Christ Jesus, that you were enriched in everything by Him in all utterance and all knowledge, even as the testimony of Christ was confirmed in you, so that you come short in no gift, eagerly waiting for the revelation of our Lord Jesus Christ, who will also confirm you to the end, that you may be blameless in the day of our Lord Jesus Christ.* (1 Corinthians 1:4–8)

With all the problems in that church, it took some faith on Paul's part to believe that the Corinthians could be *"blameless in the day of our Lord Jesus Christ."* But Paul believed for them, saying,

> *God is faithful, by whom you were called into the fellowship of His Son, Jesus Christ our Lord.* (verse 9)

In contrast, when Paul wrote to the Galatians, who didn't have any obvious moral problems—no drunkenness, no immorality, and evidently no quarrels or divisions—he was not pleased. In a way, these believers were leading very good lives—*legalistically*. But Paul was much more upset about the legalism of the Galatians than he was about the sins of the Corinthians. In Paul's introductory comments, he does not say a single word of thanksgiving to God for the grace He has given to them or for all the good He has done for them. Instead, he writes:

> *I marvel that you are turning away so soon from Him who called you in the grace of Christ, to a different gospel, which is not another; but there are some who trouble you and want to pervert the gospel of Christ.* (Galatians 1:6–7)

The problem that made Paul so upset—or, as we would say in modern English, so "hot under the collar"—was *legalism*. In our next chapters, we will explore some of the reasons why legalism is so dangerous to our faith.

17

THE "CARNAL" NATURE

To comprehend the subtleties of the snare of legalism, we must understand certain terms in Scripture. Through the years, I have discovered there are some biblical words that need further clarification if we are going to truly understand the message the Word of God is conveying.

In the New Testament, a phrase we often come across is *"the flesh."* Most Christians have a vague idea of what this term signifies, but in this chapter, we will closely examine its meaning. The *New International Version* tends to translate it as the *"sinful nature."* However, in my opinion, that expression obscures what Paul means by "the flesh" when he uses this phrase in his writings.

OUR REBEL NATURE

As I understand it, "the flesh" is the nature every human being has inherited by descent from the fallen Adam. Remember, Adam had no descendants until after he had become a rebel. Therefore, every one of his descendants now has within him the nature of a rebel. That is the nature of "the flesh."

Paul sometimes uses the word *flesh* to refer to the physical body. (In each case, we have to consider the context to determine his particular meaning.) However, when Paul uses this term in Galatians, he is not talking about the human body. He is referring to the inherited rebel nature. The Bible also refers to this rebel nature as the *"old man."* (See, for example, Romans 6:6.)

Like it or not, we need to understand the nature of the flesh, our rebel nature. In modern English, we have the word *fleshly*, but that is not a word we normally see in Scripture. What is the word used in the Bible to describe the sin nature of our "flesh"? *"Carnal."* (See, for example, 1 Corinthians 3:3.) If you know anything about the Romance languages, all of them have a word for "meat" or "flesh" that is directly related to the Latin word *carnis*. Therefore, "carnal" refers to the flesh—our flesh. I don't object to using the translation "fleshly," but I think it is more correct to use the term "carnal."

SEEKING INDEPENDENCE FROM GOD

What can we say about this rebel, carnal nature we inherited from Adam? The essence of the carnal nature is this: *the desire to be independent from God.* My personal conviction is that when God has finished His purposes for our world and brings this age to a close, there will be nothing and no one in heaven or on earth who is independent from Him. Those who want to remain independent from God will have been confined to a place Jesus calls *"outer darkness"* (Matthew 8:12; 22:13; 25:30).

You see, most of us don't naturally grasp the appalling sinfulness of the desire to be independent from God. God created this universe, and as far as the Bible reveals, there are only two types of created beings that have ever wanted to be independent from Him. The first was a group of angels; the second was the human race. No other created entity in the universe—the stars, the animals, the seas—seeks to operate independently of God. They all depend on Him. The root problem of humanity is this inherited desire to be independent from its Creator.

I have often counseled people who came to me from halfway around the world seeking an answer to their problems. Many times, I have said to them, "Listen, travel will never get you away from your problem, because wherever you travel, you take the problem with you. Your problem is *in* you. It is the inner nature that desires to be independent from God."

When Satan tempted Adam and Eve in the garden of Eden, he said, in effect, "If you eat of this tree, you will be like God." (See Genesis 3:1–5.)

There is nothing wrong with a desire to be like God. That is a very good desire. The issue was that Adam and Eve wanted to be like God *without depending on Him*.

THE PROBLEM WITH "RELIGION"

The desire to be independent from God is the root problem of humanity. And the universal method humanity uses to try to attain this independence is "religion." We think, "If I just keep all these rules, and if I attend a church, mosque, or temple, that's all I need to do." This kind of thinking is erroneous. Following a set of rules will not make you independent from God. The very desire to be independent from Him, which is often expressed in religion, is the root of all our problems.

Sometimes that rebel in us can be very religious. He can use a lot of spiritual language. But he is still a rebel. Let's see what Paul says about the flesh in Romans 8:8:

So then, those who are in the flesh cannot please God.

There is nothing you can ever do in your fleshly nature to please God, because you are acting out of rebellion. However, we have learned that God has provided a different way of achieving righteousness, which is not by keeping a set of rules or by being religious—it is by *believing*.

A DIFFERENT WAY

In a passage from the fourth chapter of Romans, which we looked at briefly in an earlier chapter of this book, Paul makes a most amazing point. In this passage, he refers to the example of Abraham, who is the father of all who believe, and discusses how Abraham was justified:

What then shall we say that Abraham our father has found according to the flesh? For if Abraham was justified by works, he has something to boast about, but not before God. For what does the Scripture say? "Abraham believed God, and it was accounted to him for righteousness." (Romans 4:1–3)

Please notice it was not what Abraham *did* that made him righteous. It was his *believing* that was *"accounted to him for righteousness."* Paul continues this amazing point in verses 4–5:

> *Now to him who works, the wages are not counted as grace but as debt. But to him who does not work but believes on Him who justifies the ungodly, his faith is accounted for righteousness.*

What is the first requirement for your faith to be accounted as righteousness? You have to stop "working": *"to him who does not work."* We must come to the end of every attempt to earn righteousness with God by what we do. If you have not come to this point, you have never really entered into the provision of the grace of God through the gospel. I would guess that maybe 50 percent of professing Christians have never actually come to the place where they have said, "There is nothing I can do to earn God's favor, to achieve righteousness. I have to stop trying."

Can you accept this statement: *"To him who does not work but believes on Him who justifies the ungodly, his faith is accounted for righteousness"*? As long as you are trying to earn God's approval, your faith is not accounted for righteousness. Righteousness does not come by faith plus works—it comes by faith alone.

The reason Paul was so upset with the Galatians was that they had lost sight of this principle of "faith alone." They had reverted to religion and legalism as their means of achieving righteousness. Religion is pride's way of saying, "I don't need God. I can make it on my own through my own set of rules and my own way of doing things."

Let me just say that it is very difficult to give up following the rules of one's religion. Somehow, it feels "safe" to always know exactly what one is supposed to do. But that leaves no room at all to be led by the Holy Spirit. When we are living according to religion, we think we don't need Him because we have our rules to tell us what to do.

In the next chapter, we will find out what it means to take a leap of faith—to let go of rules, religion, and legalism, and to be led instead by the Person of the Holy Spirit.

18

DEPENDING UPON THE SPIRIT

If we are not made righteous by keeping a set of rules, then how are we made righteous? What is the way of righteousness the New Testament prescribes? It is stated very simply in Romans 8:14:

For as many as are led by the Spirit of God, these are sons of God.

In the original Greek, the word translated as *"sons"* here refers to mature sons, not little children. What is the mark of a mature son or daughter of God? Keeping a set of rules? No. Being led by the Holy Spirit.

In this verse, Paul uses the continuing present tense: *"As many as are* [continually being] *led by the Spirit of God,"* they, and they alone, *"are sons of God."* The only way you can live as a mature child of God is to be continually led by the Holy Spirit.

This is the essence of the Christian life—being led by the Spirit. When you are led by the Holy Spirit, you are not independent. You depend upon Him moment by moment.

OPPOSING FORCES

We cannot have it both ways—we either work for our own righteousness or we are led by the Holy Spirit. It is either one or the other. You have to decide which one you will choose. Galatians 5:16 says,

*I say then: Walk in the Spirit, and you shall not fulfill the lust of the
flesh.*

Let me emphasize here that the remedy for lust is *not* a set of rules.
The more you fight lust, the more power it has over you. You find yourself
trying to overcome lust by thinking, "I must not lust. I must not think this
way. I must not look at those pictures. I must not, I must not, I must not."
Yet, the more you say "I must not," the more lust dominates your thinking.
What is the solution? To walk in the Spirit. Paul goes on to say:

*For the flesh lusts against the Spirit, and the Spirit against the flesh;
and these are contrary to one another, so that you do not do the things
that you wish. But if you are led by the Spirit, you are not under the
law.* (Galatians 5:17–18)

The fleshly nature and the Holy Spirit are in opposition to one another. They will never work together. Clearly, we have to decide how we want
to live. We cannot be under the law and be led by the Spirit at the same
time. We have to make a choice.

"WILL THE SPIRIT LEAD ME?"

Many people think being led by the Spirit is a very uncertain way to
live. They feel it is too risky, thinking, "Can I really trust the Holy Spirit
to lead me?" Before I tell you what I believe the Holy Spirit will do for you
if you decide to trust Him, let me offer you an analogy that might help to
illustrate my point.

For me, the Bible is like a piano. A piano has a certain number of white
keys, a certain number of black keys, certain octaves and pedals. However,
on its own, it doesn't produce music. But if a brilliant pianist were to sit
down and begin to play on that piano, he would produce marvelous music
that others could enjoy. Similarly, the Bible has a fixed number of books
and is complete from beginning to end. But on its own, there is no "music."
When I was unsaved, the prospect of reading the Bible was like looking at
a piano without a pianist. Nothing came out of it.

Who is the Bible's "pianist"? The Holy Spirit. It is wonderful to have a Bible; but we are dependent on the Holy Spirit to enable us to understand what God is saying to us through His Word. God doesn't expect us to manage without His Spirit, because there is no substitute for Him.

HOW THE SPIRIT HELPS US

There are three ways the Holy Spirit will lead you in your relationship to the Scriptures. First, He will draw you to the Word of God. Do you remember when you were born again by the Holy Spirit? Did you gain an insatiable appetite for reading the Bible? Who gave you that appetite? The Holy Spirit.

Second, the Holy Spirit will interpret the Word of God for you. He is the Author of the Bible, and we cannot understand the Word without Him. Therefore, if you want to know what the Bible means, ask the Author. He will tell you.

Third, the Holy Spirit will show you how to apply God's Word. There are many parts of the Bible that can seem rather obscure when you first read them. But the Holy Spirit can be your interpreter. He will show you how to apply those verses—just ask Him.

FRIENDSHIP WITH THE SPIRIT

I believe the Bible is essential for the Christian life. It is totally true, authoritative, and reliable. However, I also believe in the Holy Spirit and His role in teaching and guiding us. The Holy Spirit will direct you to God's Word, interpret the Word, and show you how to apply it in your life.

Dependence upon the Holy Spirit is not an option. Cultivate a friendship with Him. He is not just half of a phrase at the end of the Apostle's Creed. He is not a mere theological abstraction. He is a Person, just as much as God the Father is a Person and God the Son is a Person. You will never have a better friend in life than the Holy Spirit.

WHAT THE SPIRIT DOES *NOT* DO

You should know there are two things the Holy Spirit will never lead you to do. First, as the author of Scripture, He will never lead you to do anything contrary to God's Word. He never contradicts Himself. This is one reason why you need to read and study your Bible—so you can check if what you feel the Holy Spirit is saying to you is consistent with Scripture. If it does not line up, it is not from the Holy Spirit.

Second, the Holy Spirit will never lead you to do anything contrary to His own nature. His nature is holy. Please, don't be afraid to look to the Holy Spirit. You may feel it is a big risk to do this, but it is a much bigger risk *not* to seek Him. The Christian life is lived by faith. There is no way of living the life of a Christian without some risks.

A PERSONAL GUIDE

Let me give you my favorite illustration to explain the difference between following a set of rules and being led by the Holy Spirit. Suppose you have to find your way to a certain destination. You have never been there before, and you have two alternatives: one is a map (the law), and the other is a personal guide (the Holy Spirit).

Whenever I give this illustration, I always picture a young university graduate who has earned his degree and is pretty pleased with himself. God says to him, "Which do you want—the map or the Guide?" He thinks for a moment and then replies, "I'm pretty well-educated, I have a good understanding of life now, and I know how to read a map. Give me the map."

So, off he goes with the map. The way is clear, the sun is shining, the birds are singing, and he thinks to himself, "This is a piece of cake!" But about thirty-six hours later, it is dark, it is raining, he is in the middle of a forest, and he doesn't know whether he is facing north, south, east, or west. Suddenly, a gentle voice says, "Can I help you?"

He replies, "Oh, Holy Spirit, I need You!" The Holy Spirit takes him by the hand, leads him out of the forest, and puts him on the right path. Then they continue along together. But after a while, the young graduate says to himself, "Well, that was pretty dumb. I could have made it on my own—I didn't really need to get so nervous." He turns around, and the personal Guide is no longer there. So, he decides, "I'll keep going on my own." About forty-eight hours later, do you know where he is? In the middle of a bog. And with every step, he sinks deeper into the quagmire.

Again, a gentle voice says to him, "Perhaps you need Me now." Relieved, he pleads, "Oh, Holy Spirit, pull me out of this!" After being rescued, he starts off again with the Holy Spirit at his side. After a while, coming to a crossroads, the young man turns to his Guide and says, "You know, I've got a map here. Maybe that would help." The Holy Spirit responds, "I don't need the map. I know the way. Besides, I'm the One who drew the map." Then He begins to interpret the map to the young graduate.

Without the Holy Spirit as your guide, your map (the law) will not lead you to your destination. You will only end up in a dense forest or a bog, having lost your way.

19

LAW AND GRACE

Even though, in Christ, we are no longer under the law as a means of righteousness, we cannot say we don't need "law." We need to understand what law will do for us and what it will not do for us.

When I say "law," I am not talking about the law of Moses, or the first five books of the Old Testament. I am referring to rules and laws in a general sense. It might be government law or the rules of a church denomination or particular congregation. In this sense, law has two primary functions.

FUNCTIONS OF THE LAW

First, law defines and restrains evil by setting boundaries. With the breakdown of law today, especially moral law in the West, ethical boundaries are being abolished. There are really no limits to what people can do, which has resulted in an increase in lawlessness.

Second, law enables people to live in harmony with one another. If there were no law, citizens in a society could not function together safely and peaceably. The general principle is that if we are going to live together with others, we have to agree on and keep certain protocols. Let me give a simple example. Consider basic traffic laws. In America, motorists drive on the right-hand side of the road; in England, they drive on the left-hand side. It doesn't matter which side of the road a country chooses to have its motorists drive on. However, if a particular motorist doesn't know which side everyone else in the country is driving on, he or she may be in big trouble!

Here's another example: in a family, the parents are obligated to make certain simple rules about bedtime for the children, keeping the house clean, and showing respect and courtesy to other family members. Otherwise, a household could quickly become chaotic and unhealthy.

Laws and rules such as these are necessary to define and restrain wrong behavior and for the proper functioning of families, organizations, and society in general. But we must realize that laws and rules cannot make us righteous.

INADEQUATE FOR CHRISTIAN LIVING

In this regard, let's consider the rules of church denominations and individual congregations. In my view, if you belong to a particular denomination or church, you should respect and abide by its rules. If you can't do this, you probably shouldn't be in that particular group.

However, be aware that most church rules (there might be exceptions) don't really deal with the basic issues of Christian community, such as love, forgiveness, and relationships. They deal with secondary issues, such as abstinence from sexual relations before marriage and the types of dress and entertainment that are appropriate. They give the impression that keeping these rules is all you need to do to be in right standing with God. This is why law-keeping can be so deceptive.

Jesus's statements from the Sermon on the Mount clearly demonstrate why religious rules are inadequate for Christian living:

"Blessed are the poor in spirit" (Matthew 5:3). Do church rules tend to make you "poor in spirit?" Do they cause you to have a heart that seeks God, acknowledging your need for Him? Usually, religious rules have the opposite effect in our lives.

"Blessed are the meek" (verse 5). How many church rules produce meekness, or humbleness?

"*Blessed are those who hunger and thirst for righteousness*" (verse 6). Do the rules of a church make you hungry and thirsty for righteousness?

"*Blessed are the merciful*" (verse 7). Most church rules don't demand mercy (although some may).

"*Blessed are the pure in heart*" (verse 8). Church rules cannot make your heart pure.

"*Blessed are the peacemakers*" (verse 9). Generally speaking, the churches with the most rules have the most fights! Is that not true? If you were to examine the most legalistic church denominations, you would see evidence of numerous divisions that have taken place. Why? Because they attach everything to their rules. When you are living by rules, you have to keep on making more and more rules.

THE END RESULT OF RULES

When we depend solely on religious or moral laws, two unfortunate results normally follow. First, they promote self-righteousness and pride, as illustrated by Jesus's parable of the Pharisee and the tax collector:

Two men went up to the temple to pray, one a Pharisee and the other a tax collector. The Pharisee stood and prayed thus with himself, "God, I thank You that I am not like other men—extortioners, unjust, adulterers, or even as this tax collector. I fast twice a week; I give tithes of all that I possess." And the tax collector, standing afar off, would not so much as raise his eyes to heaven, but beat his breast, saying, "God, be merciful to me a sinner!" I tell you, this man [the tax collector] went down to his house justified rather than the other. (Luke 18:10–14)

Tax collectors were outcasts of Jewish society. So, in the eyes of a Jewish audience, this man was the lowest of the low. Please notice that the Pharisee prayed "*with himself.*" He was not praying to God—he was praying to himself. Which of these two men achieved righteousness? Not the Pharisee, with his laws, but the tax collector, with a cry for mercy. Basically, keeping religious rules will make you proud.

Second, keeping religious or moral laws distracts us from the primary issues and causes us to focus on peripheral matters. Note what Jesus said in Matthew 23:23 to the Pharisees, who are the biblical example of people who live according to religious rules:

> *Woe to you, scribes and Pharisees, hypocrites! For you pay tithe of mint and anise and cummin, and have neglected the weightier matters of the law: justice and mercy and faith. These you ought to have done, without leaving the others undone.*

Jesus did not say it is wrong to pay tithes of mint, anise, and cummin. But the Pharisees were so caught up with their rules about tithes that they were oblivious to the claims of justice, mercy, and faith—the issues of the heart that really matter.

THE PRIMARY ISSUE

The primary issue, which we identified at the beginning of this book, is love. *"The goal of our instruction is love"* (1 Timothy 1:5 NASB). Anything that deviates from this is *"idle talk"* (1 Timothy 1:6), or *"fruitless discussion"* (NASB). How many churches really focus on love? How many churches have rules that (if it were possible) are designed to produce love in their people?

We could probably agree that basically, with only a few exceptions, the most legalistic people are also the most unloving people. This is not an accident—it is an example of cause and effect. It is what legalism does. It elevates performance over love and mercy.

20

EFFECTIVE GRACE

The only alternative to legalism is grace. What is grace? I could give you a theological definition, such as "Grace is the favor of God toward the undeserving and the ill-deserving." There is nothing wrong with that definition, but it doesn't make grace sound very exciting.

Grace is intangible—but it is absolutely real and extremely powerful. It is a power. It is supernatural. I have said many times that "grace begins where human ability ends." As long as you think you can handle life yourself, you won't seek the grace of God. But when you come to the end of all your resources, grace is a supernatural resource that is available to you.

MUTUALLY EXCLUSIVE

Law and grace are mutually exclusive. Paul makes this truth very clear in a startling statement in the sixth chapter of Romans:

> *For sin shall not have dominion over you, for you are not under law but under grace.* (Romans 6:14)

There are two logical implications of this verse. First, you can't be under both law and grace at the same time. You can't combine them, and you can't have them both. You have to make up your mind and choose one or the other.

Second, if you are under law, sin *will* have dominion over you. You don't have a choice in the matter. Do you accept that statement? Is it a fair interpretation of the above Scripture? In another teaching, Paul says,

> *The strength of sin is the law.*   (1 Corinthians 15:56)

This is an amazing statement also. If we really think about it, what does it mean? When you live under the law, it is standing in front of you all the time, like a huge, immovable stone tablet with the Ten Commandments engraved on it. It is outside you. It is external. If you say to yourself, "I'm going to keep that law," what are you relying on? You are relying on your own strength.

Many Christians begin in grace but end in law. They go back to keeping rules because it is natural for human beings to try to rely on their own ability and efforts. But when you do that, you "reactivate" the "old man" who died when you came to Christ. You begin to live according to the carnal nature again.

Let's review Paul's words from Romans 6:14. I hope you will carefully consider them and how they can affect the way you live.

> *For sin shall not have dominion over you, for you are not under law but under grace.*

May I ask you a question? Please consider it carefully. Are you living according to law or according to grace? Remember that it is not one *and* the other. It is one *or* the other. You have to choose.

GRACE IS WITH YOU

I want to try to give you an appetite for grace. Why? Because there are no words to express how wonderful, how totally desirable, how inestimably precious is the grace of God! We will read two passages from Paul's epistles to the Corinthians. In 1 Corinthians, Paul compares himself with those who were apostles before him:

For I am the least of the apostles, who am not worthy to be called an apostle, because I persecuted the church of God. But by the grace of God I am what I am, and His grace toward me was not in vain; but I labored more abundantly than they all, yet not I, but the grace of God which was with me. (1 Corinthians 15:9–10)

The word *"grace"* occurs three times in this passage. To paraphrase, Paul is saying, "I didn't deserve anything. I was the worst. I was the chief of sinners. (See 1 Timothy 1:15.) But God chose to demonstrate His grace in me—and by His grace I am what I am. His grace was not bestowed upon me in vain. By His grace, I have labored abundantly. Yet it wasn't my work at all, but the grace of God that *'was with me'.*" Can you see that grace is not just a theological abstraction? It is *with* you, and it is infinitely powerful and inexhaustibly rich.

GOD'S GRACE IS SUFFICIENT

Then, in 2 Corinthians, Paul speaks about a problem he could not solve—one that God would not solve for him. It can be really discouraging when you know God *could* resolve an issue, but He *doesn't.* This is what Paul says:

And lest I should be exalted above measure by the abundance of the revelations [In one word, what was the problem God was guarding Paul against? *Pride*], *a thorn in the flesh was given to me, a messenger of Satan to buffet me, lest I be exalted above measure.* (2 Corinthians 12:7)

Here is my personal theory about the nature of Paul's *"thorn in the flesh."* I believe there was a satanic principality or power that had just one assignment—to make trouble for Paul. The trouble this apostle went through was absolutely unnatural. Wherever he went, a riot or uproar ensued. He usually ended up being put into prison, beaten, or chased out of the city. It didn't happen to all the other apostles. They certainly had their share of problems—but there seemed to be something totally unnatural about what Paul went through. In 2 Corinthians 12:7, he says, in effect, "An agent of Satan was sent to buffet me, with no other job but to make trouble for me. Wherever I went, he went too, and stirred up trouble." Paul continues,

> *Concerning this thing I pleaded with the Lord three times that it might depart from me.*   (2 Corinthians 12:8)

Not once, not twice, but three times Paul pleaded with the Lord to get this opponent off his back. But God said to him,

> *My grace is sufficient for you, for My strength is made perfect in weakness.*   (verse 9)

In essence, God was saying to Paul, "All you need is My grace. It is never lacking. It is always sufficient." Do you start and end each day with problems like Paul describes? Maybe you have prayed, fasted, and done everything else you know to do in order to resolve a particular problem. Let me just say to you, "God's grace is sufficient—just as it was for Paul."

Those of us in ministry can't solve everybody's problems. Sometimes we can't even solve our own! But God's grace is sufficient for each and every one of us who trusts in Him.

GOD'S GRACE STRENGTHENS US

In the second half of 2 Corinthians 12:9, Paul makes another remarkable statement:

> *Therefore most gladly I will rather boast in my infirmities, that the power of Christ may rest upon me.*

I have read this verse hundreds of times, and I have often had to admit to God, "Lord, I know Paul said this, and I know it is in the Bible—but I can't honestly say it myself."

Paul goes on to say,

Therefore I take pleasure [note that] *in infirmities, in reproaches, in needs, in persecutions, in distresses, for Christ's sake. For when I am weak, then I am strong.*   (2 Corinthians 12:10)

What made Paul strong when he was weak? The grace of God. Can you say, *"I take pleasure in infirmities, in reproaches, in needs, in persecutions, in distresses"*? I know I am a lot nearer to being able to say this than I used to be, partly through observing my wife Ruth, who has suffered over several years with various debilitating physical problems. God came to her help on various occasions, sometimes with miraculous healings. Even though the problems were not all resolved, I observed the increasing grace of God in her life. Two of the worst situations for her condition are air travel and sitting in meetings. If she had to choose a way of life, the activities we need to participate in to conduct our ministry would be the last options she would select. Many women would have said, "Well, God hasn't healed me, so I'm just giving up." However, she didn't say that. Why? Because of the grace of God.

When you get to the absolute bottom, that is when God's grace is the most magnanimous. He will always make His grace available to you. He will never withhold it. God is not poor in grace. He has enough for everybody—and plenty to spare. Why would you revert to living according to a mere set of rules when you can have the grace of God?

WHY GO BACK?

As we close this chapter and this section of *The Coming Revival,* I trust I have been able to give you a desire to live according to the grace of God. I trust I have provided enough of a taste for you to accept His grace when the going is toughest and when your need is greatest.

Perhaps you or someone close to you is in an extremely difficult situation. In our troubled world, so many people are in unbearable situations involving family challenges, health problems, strained relationships, or other issues. I commend you to the grace of God—because His grace is sufficient. He wants believers to be a demonstration to the whole world of what His grace can do in human lives.

Ruth and I once had a young woman working for us who had been a prostitute, a drug addict, and an unwed mother. She had been such a bad mother that social services had taken her child away from her. But after she received Christ, if you hadn't know her past, you wouldn't have believed what she had once been. All of that was behind her. She became pure and radiant in every aspect of her life.

That is the grace of God. We must not cheat ourselves by settling for less than His grace! The Lord has always been willing to give His grace. If you have never fully yielded to the grace of God, if you have never really let God's grace into your life, I urge you to do so.

Perhaps you have been holding back due to unbelief, self-centeredness, or even self-confidence. You have never opened up—you have never really come to the place of asking for grace. Can you understand that if you are to be made righteous, the first step you have to take is to stop *trying* to be righteous?

God's grace begins when you come to the end of all your own efforts. If you are willing, if you want to stop relying on your own strength, if you have come to the end of yourself and are ready to start trusting in God's beautiful gift of grace, please pray this prayer:

Dear Heavenly Father,

I am at the end of myself. I confess to You that I have lived under the law, trying to become righteous by my own efforts. I no longer want to live this way—I want to be led by the Holy Spirit.

I want my life to reflect Your grace and glory. I relinquish control of my life, and I receive Your grace now. According to Your Word, I have been saved through faith, not of myself—it is a gift from You. I thank You, I trust You, and I love You. In Jesus's name. Amen.

PART FIVE:

UNMASKING WITCHCRAFT

21

REMOVING THE STONES

want to begin part five with a word of encouragement. In the Bible, there is a particularly beautiful Scripture about building a highway to revival:

> Go through, go through the gates! Prepare the way for the people; build up, build up the highway! Take out the stones, lift up a banner for the peoples! (Isaiah 62:10)

BOULDERS IN THE WAY

Note the phrase *"take out the stones."* I believe that over the centuries, the enemy has planted great boulders where the highway to revival is to be built. These boulders are intended to stand in the way of God's people. He wants to keep us discouraged and unbelieving—and he will do anything to prevent us from aligning ourselves with the will of God. But I believe God is going to drive out our enemy and give us the power to destroy him. One of the tasks before us is to *"take out the stones"* so the highway may be prepared.

What I have shared thus far should help prepare us for this task. That is why, in the previous two sections of this book, I have exposed what I believe are two of the greatest boulders hindering revival. The first is pride and the second is legalism. It is my hope that these chapters have served as a sort of crowbar—beginning the process of loosening the boulders so that

God's people, working together, can remove what is blocking the highway to revival.

We continue our study now with the third hindrance, which is a powerful and threatening spiritual force: witchcraft. Some of what I am going to share may be puzzling or even somewhat shocking to you. However, I want to assure you that even if you are a little offended by certain aspects of this discussion, I am speaking out of deep love and concern for your well-being. What I describe does not come from theory but from extensive experience in dealing with this topic.

BORN TO RULE

For many years now, I have been involved in "Unmasking Witchcraft." That process begins by understanding God's plan for humanity to rule the earth—and why it went wrong. When God created the first human beings, He gave them the authority to govern the world on His behalf:

So God created man in His own image; in the image of God He created him; male and female He created them. Then God blessed them, and said to them, "Be fruitful and multiply; fill the earth and subdue it; have dominion over the fish of the sea, over the birds of the air, and over every living thing that moves on the earth." (Genesis 1:27–28)

God created man to be His "viceroy" on earth. Let me explain this title in case you are unfamiliar with it. I was born in India in 1915. At that time, there was an official there called a *viceroy* who represented the British monarch. In much the same way, man was intended to be God's representative on earth. We were meant to exercise His authority in accordance with His revealed will and plan. This commission and place of dominion were born into our very nature.

However, when human beings fell into rebellion and sin, they lost their authority, because authority is only given by God to those who are obedient. However, humanity did not lose the inner urge to dominate. Unfortunately, when humans dominate in their fallen condition, they don't do it by the authority of God. Instead, they do it by an alien spiritual power that has supplanted the place of God in their lives. The name for this power is *witchcraft*. Witchcraft is anything that usurps the true authority of God and seeks to dominate and control others in its place.

IMPROPER CONTROL

The key word in dealing with witchcraft is *control*. "Control" can be a neutral term. However, in the sense that I am using it for the purposes of this book, it has a sinister meaning. I don't believe God ever controls anybody. He has given each of us a free will, and He expects us to cooperate with Him on the basis of that will. However, He does not control us and make us do things contrary to our own will.

Perhaps you have been in a worship service or another church meeting when someone has stood up, said something ludicrous, and then claimed, "The Holy Spirit made me say that." The truth of the matter is this: *the Holy Spirit never makes us do anything.* He never overrides human free will, because God has given us free will as a gift, and He respects the free will God has given us. Anybody who says the Holy Spirit "made me" behave in a certain way is talking about a spirit that is *not* the Holy Spirit.

Satan, on the other hand, will seek to control. He will try to override human will. If he can, he will take control of a human personality and put that individual in a mental state where they absolutely don't know what they are doing. The person may come to themselves hours later and discover they have done things they never intended to do.

God never deals with us in this way. Basically, whenever you are confronted by something that seeks to control you against your will, you are face-to-face with witchcraft.

THE BASIS OF WITCHCRAFT

The book of 1 Samuel gives us a revelation of the basis of witchcraft. It describes how King Saul, Israel's first king, disobeyed a direct command of the Lord and instead followed his own inclinations. In doing so, he usurped God's authority. When Samuel the prophet confronted King Saul about this, he said to him,

For rebellion is as the sin of witchcraft.   (1 Samuel 15:23)

Many biblical translations use the word "*divination*" rather than "*witchcraft*" in this verse. Actually, there are three different aspects of the same evil power: (1) There is *witchcraft*, which is the power element. (2) There is *divination*, which is the revelatory element seen most commonly in fortune-telling. (3) There is *sorcery*, which uses certain items or objects to control people. Part of our discussion in this section will be an examination of all three of these ways in which witchcraft operates.

First Samuel 15:23 tells us that witchcraft is the result of rebellion. Wherever you find rebellion, you can expect to find witchcraft, because they are twins. Today, we are essentially living in a rebellious society that has deliberately rejected the righteous government of God in the person of Jesus Christ. What has been the result? Our whole society is pervaded with witchcraft. This is a spiritual reality the church can no longer ignore. However, there is no need to shrink back, because we have this promise: "*He will drive out your enemies before you, saying, "Destroy them!"* (Deuteronomy 33:27 NIV).

In the next few chapters, we will look at the universal ways witchcraft functions in different areas of society—in the culture, in social institutions such as the family, and even in the church itself. We will start with a general overview, beginning with witchcraft as it has existed for centuries in undeveloped cultures of the world.

22

WITCHCRAFT IN UNDEVELOPED CULTURES

Witchcraft is what I call "the religion of fallen man." It is found everywhere on earth, in every nation. It takes different forms, but you will find basic similarities in all the so-called primitive religions. In each expression of witchcraft, the object is to control, and there are specific areas witchcraft seeks to control.

AREAS OF CONTROL

First, witchcraft endeavors to control the forces of nature. Many tribal nations have what they call "rainmakers"—witchdoctors who try to cause rain to fall. Along with seeking to "make rain," they may also seek to control crops or produce fruitfulness in their region. The ultimate aim, however, is control over natural elements.

Second, witchcraft seeks to control the course of life, particularly the ability to bring forth children. In 1987, Ruth and I were in Zambia in a large meeting of about seven thousand indigenous people. Nearly all of them were professing church members. When it came time for ministry, one of the needs we prayed for was barrenness. About two hundred women assembled in front of us. But my interpreter, who knew his own people very well, would not let us pray until he asked a question: "How many of you have been to the witchdoctor for a potion to cure barrenness?" Amazingly, there were only two out of two hundred women who did *not* put up their hands. That gives you some idea of the influence witchdoctors and shamans have in many of these cultures.

Third, witchcraft seeks to control other human beings—to get someone to do what another individual wants them to do. One particular way witchcraft is often used for this purpose is to influence a man to marry a particular woman. The woman sees a man she wants to marry. So, she goes to the witchdoctor, obtains a potion, and somehow gets the man to take the potion. She is convinced that once he has done so, he will fall in love with her.

Those are just three out of many possible examples. But I want to you to understand that the aim is always the same—control. And the power is always evil. Do not for a moment imagine that only God works supernaturally. The devil has enormous supernatural power, and much of the power exercised in witchcraft is supernatural—and it is evil.

COUNTERFEITS OF TRUE RELIGION

Witchcraft has various supernatural manifestations. In a certain sense, these tend to be counterfeits of the covenants God has made with humanity—first through the law of Moses and then through the death of Jesus Christ. Let's consider some of the ways witchcraft tries to copy true, God-given religion.

SACRIFICES

Animal sacrifices are a normal part of most witchcraft. Sometimes this may include human sacrifice. This is not something out of the dark past, nor is it limited to only primitive cultures. In the United States, human sacrifices take place through witches' covens or cults.

Often the leader of the cult will impregnate a woman who is under his control and will arrange it so that the birth is never registered. Then they will sacrifice the newborn baby to Satan. I actually read an account of one young woman in a cult who gave birth to a baby, after which the cult leader placed a dagger in her hand, held her hand in his, and made her plunge the dagger into her own child. So again, this is not something only from the remote past or so-called primitive lands. It is taking place widely all over the world—even in modern societies.

COVENANTS AND OATHS

Witchcraft also uses covenants and oaths. God Himself instituted covenants and oaths in the Old Testament. But in witchcraft, covenants are made between people who are in covens or other satanic groups. One of witchcraft's most powerful instruments is curses, something in which it specializes. There is real power in satanic curses. Never discount this reality or say it couldn't happen to you. In my book *Blessing or Curse: You Can Choose*, I include examples of satanic curses that nearly ruined people's lives.

We must understand that this battle is not being fought on the natural plane. It is being fought on the supernatural plane. The power of God is supernatural, and the power of Satan is supernatural. Although God's power is infinitely greater, the servants of Satan do wield supernatural power, and the servants of God need divine supernatural power to combat it.

SPELLS AND INCANTATIONS

These dark forces also use spells and incantations against people. If you are familiar with the increase in witchcraft around the world, you are aware that incantation is a very common expression of witchcraft. Many years ago, I had an unusual conversation with a man who scheduled an appointment with me. When we met, he said, "I want to apologize to you because I'm a wizard. I got angry with you because I wanted to speak to you in a meeting and you wouldn't speak to me. So, I put a curse on your family, and I want to apologize."

I'm not sure he was speaking the truth about this matter, by any means. However, he went on to boast about his accomplishments in witchcraft, which included achieving telekinesis—the ability to move objects at a distance. He described how he was able to get his name erased from a list in a locked room to which he had no access. Then he told me, "I've discovered the most powerful form of witchcraft is incantation, and that's what I'm specializing in now."

DRUGS AND MUSIC

Witchcraft also uses drugs and music. Most of the illegal drugs we hear so much about today play some role in the practice of sorcery. Remember, sorcery uses certain objects or items to gain control of people.

The hard rock culture, with its associated drugs, is a perfect example of sorcery. From what I understand, the compelling drumbeat in Africa that found its way to the West via South America has been an instrument of sorcery, or witchcraft, for hundreds and hundreds of years. The real achievement of a witchdoctor is to know how to have people taken over by a demon. At one time, when a tribe went out to battle against another, the witchdoctor's function was to get his tribe so filled with demons that they were undefeatable. Along with potions, one of the main methods of drawing demons was the use of music, which included a heavy, unrelenting drumbeat.

Every parent needs to take note that when you encounter what is called hard rock and recreational drugs, you are encountering some expression of sorcery. That is the right name for it. Anywhere there is witchcraft, you will find an atmosphere of fear and darkness. It pervades the whole scene.

"CURSES: CAUSE AND CURE"

Throughout this section, I will offer illustrations, such as the one I'm about to share, to prove to you that witchcraft operates supernaturally.

Some years ago, Ruth and I met a Jewish lady in South Africa who had received Jesus as her Messiah. This woman personally told us the following story. At one time in her life, both of her hands had become completely crippled with rheumatoid arthritis, causing continual pain, to the point that she lost the use of her hands. A Christian friend visited her and said, "I have three cassette tapes for you to listen to." They were three of my recorded messages entitled "Curses: Cause and Cure."

This Jewish lady was a rather sophisticated person, and she really did not believe in curses. She considered them to be remnants of the Middle Ages. However, because her friend had asked her to, she listened to all three cassettes. At the very end, where I was about to lead people in a prayer by which they could release themselves from a curse, the cassette jammed! It would not go forward, it would not go back, and it would not eject. (I don't believe that was a natural occurrence—it was supernatural.)

So the woman said to her friend, "Well, then, I can't say the prayer."

But the friend replied, "Oh yes, you can, because I had it typed out. Even if you can't listen to it, you can read it."

Her friend went and got the typed copy. It was a simple prayer that would not take as much as three minutes to read. The woman read this prayer more out of a desire to please her friend than out of any other motive. She had no concept of seeking healing—she was just dutifully reading the prayer for release from a curse. But by the time she had finished, her fingers had completely uncoiled and she was totally free from pain. Later, her doctor confirmed she no longer had rheumatoid arthritis. Think of the lengths to which the devil had gone to prevent this woman from saying a prayer that would lead to her healing!

Thus, with witchcraft, we are dealing with supernatural forces that have a measure of control over events. They don't have total control, but they have much more control than most of us are willing to recognize.

What we have been discussing so far is what I would call "pagan" witchcraft. However, we must come to terms with the fact that witchcraft can also disguise itself in Christian forms. This will be the focus of our next chapter.

23

SPIRITUAL BATTLE

Satan, through the power of witchcraft, will do everything he can to prevent the people of God from fulfilling their role as agents of revival in the world. What would be the best way for the enemy to do this? *By infiltrating the church.* Satan can do more harm to the church from inside it than he can from outside it. Therefore, it should not surprise us to realize that witchcraft has gotten into the church.

A SPIRIT OF DIVINATION

This is nothing new—the New Testament apostles themselves had to deal with witchcraft. There is a vivid example of this in the book of Acts. Paul was on a missionary journey in the city of Philippi when he encountered a *"spirit of divination."* Here is how the incident unfolded:

> *Now it happened, as we went to prayer, that a certain slave girl possessed with a spirit of divination met us, who brought her masters much profit by fortune-telling.* (Acts 16:16)

The supernatural power in fortune-telling is witchcraft. If you want to use the correct technical term for fortune-telling, it is *divination.* Actually, in the original Greek, the term translated *"spirit of divination"* is "spirit of python." The python is particularly associated with fortune-telling. This is

147

not the type of snake that poisons people. Instead, it wraps itself around people and ultimately crushes the life out of them.

A very famous medium in Washington, D.C., wrote a book in which she described the way she received her gift of divination: while she was in bed, a snake came and coiled itself around her. Would you believe that millions of Christians are gullible enough to believe her gift is from God? One of the best known charismatic preachers (whose name you would probably recognize if I told it to you) actually went to consult with her. That is an indication of the depth of deception in the church regarding witchcraft.

CONSIDER THE SOURCE

In Acts 16:16, we note that this slave girl *"brought her masters much profit by fortune-telling."* People usually don't pay money for something that doesn't work. Fortune-telling, to a certain degree, works. Before my wife Ruth was saved, while she was still living as an unconverted Jewess, she went, on the recommendation of a friend, to a fortune-teller whom she had never seen before. This fortune-teller told her three facts about her life: First, she was not able to have children of her own. Second, she had three adopted children. And third, her husband had left her. Every one of those facts was absolutely correct. But that knowledge didn't come from God—it came from Satan.

Please do not be so naive as to suppose that every time supernatural truth is presented to you, its source is God. It may easily be Satan. The Bible instructs us, *"Beloved, do not believe every spirit, but test the spirits, whether they are of God; because many false prophets have gone out into the world"* (1 John 4:1).

Let us continue the story of the encounter with the spirit of divination in Philippi:

> *This girl followed Paul and us, and cried out, saying, "These men are the servants of the Most High God, who proclaim to us the way of salvation."* (Acts 16:17)

It is interesting that every word she said was essentially true. She could not have known this information by any natural means—it was by a super-natural revelation, but its source was satanic. At first, this revelation might seem to endorse the ministry of Paul and Silas. Why would Satan want to endorse them? I believe the enemy was attempting to infiltrate the church at Philippi right from the beginning.

I can't help but believe that many contemporary missionaries, con-fronted by the same situation, would say, "Isn't this wonderful? This young woman really has discernment—she knows who we are. Let's make her a charter member of the church." However, the next verse tells us what Paul and Silas did instead:

> And this she did for many days. But Paul, greatly annoyed, turned and said to the spirit...." (Acts 16:18)

Notice that Paul did not talk to the young woman—the human in-strument through which the spirit of divination was working. He turned and spoke to the spirit, saying,

> "I command you in the name of Jesus Christ to come out of her." And he came out that very hour. (verse 18)

Once the spirit of divination had been cast out, the young slave woman could no longer tell fortunes. Her masters became angry because they had lost their source of income. (See verse 19.) The rest of Acts 16 describes how the entire city was thrown into a complete uproar. Isn't that extraor-dinary? The deliverance of one demonized young woman threw the whole city into turmoil.

In chapter 20 of this book, "Effective Grace," we discussed the partic-ular agent of Satan whose sole purpose was to buffet Paul. That demonic spirit was right on the job in this situation. He turned the whole city into an uproar, prompting the action that had Paul and Silas severely beaten and thrown into prison, merely because they had cast a demon out of a slave girl. Why was Satan so angry? Because his plan to infiltrate the church at Philippi had been foiled. Paul did not accept the slave girl's "testimony" as something from God. He recognized its source as Satan—and he categorically rejected it and dealt with it effectively.

THE FIFTH COLUMN

Although Satan's plan to infiltrate Paul and Silas's ministry didn't work, what he attempted to do is actually an established military tactic. Today, it is often called "the fifth column." Not everyone is familiar with this phrase, which has an interesting origin. It was coined in Spain in 1936. It just so happens this was the same year I hiked from France to Spain by way of the Pyrenees mountains—only to find myself in the middle of the Spanish Civil War! I quickly turned around and went back into France.

During that civil war, General Emilio Mola was besieging the city of Madrid. A journalist came to him and asked, "Tell me, general, what is your plan to take this city?" General Mola answered, "I have four columns advancing on the city. One from the north, one from the south, one from the east, and one from the west." Then he paused and said, "But it's my fifth column that I'm expecting to take the city for me." The journalist inquired, "Where is your fifth column?" The general replied, "Inside the city." That is the origin of the phrase "fifth column," defined as "a group of secret sympathizers or supporters of an enemy that engage in espionage or sabotage within defense lines or national borders."[5]

While that is the origin of the phrase, General Mola's army is not the origin of the use of this tactic. Satan has had a fifth column in the church for many hundreds of years. He and his evil spirits are at work to divide, immobilize, and destroy Christians. It is his number-one way of subverting the ministry of the church. Unfortunately, too many Christians today do not recognize the work of Satan in their midst. They are blind to the presence of Satan's "fifth column."

That is why this section of the book is called "Unmasking Witchcraft." Witchcraft, as it operates in a Christian setting and with Christian vernacular, can seem to be legitimate. Understandably, this may shock some believers. However, I want to reaffirm that I am not speaking out of theory. I am speaking out of many years of personal experience and observation

---

5. Merriam-Webster.com, 2019, https://www.merriam-webster.com/dictionary/fifth%20column.

from dealing with such situations. It took time for me to understand what I was encountering within the body of Christ. Allow me to share with you how God revealed this to me.

A DIFFERENT SPIRIT

In the first half of the 1970s in the United States, I was intensely involved in the ministry of delivering people from evil spirits. As a result of this ministry, I became not so much famous as infamous. During this period, when I was spending a large portion of my time traveling, teaching, and ministering on deliverance, strange events would take place.

For example, I would walk into a congregation, and a woman would say to me, "I don't know what is the matter with you, but when you come near me, I tremble all over." This happened several times in different congregations. Usually, the women were people of significance, such as the deacon's wife, the pastor's daughter, or the church soloist. At first, I said to myself, "Whatever is the matter with me?" Then, I said to God, "Lord, what is this?" And this is the answer He gave me: "It is witchcraft."

I said, "Lord, what do You mean by witchcraft?" I was asking God for His definition because I always think in terms of definitions. The definition He gave me is one I have used in this section to explain the nature of this evil spiritual force: "Witchcraft is the attempt to control people and get them to do what you want by the use of any spirit that is not the Holy Spirit." Then He gave me an additional insight: "If anyone has a spirit that he or she can 'use,' it is not the Holy Spirit, because the Holy Spirit is God, and *no one uses God.*"

In "Spirit-filled" groups worldwide, you will find many people who claim to "use" the Holy Spirit. I am so glad God warned me about this in advance, because I have come to learn that, even in church groups, there is sometimes a different spirit at work than the Holy Spirit. In the next chapter, we will take a closer look at witchcraft's infiltration of the body of Christ—what I call "witchcraft in disguise."

24

WITCHCRAFT IN DISGUISE

What is the purpose of a disguise? To conceal a true identity. That is the nature of witchcraft. It does not want us to know its true identity, because then we would categorically reject it. We would do what the apostle Paul did in Philippi when he cast the "python spirit" out of the fortune-telling slave girl. Even though what she was saying had a ring of truth to it—*these men are the servants of the Most High God, who proclaim to us the way of salvation*" (Acts 16:17)—the revelation was spiritually corrupt because its source was Satan. It was witchcraft in disguise.

In this chapter and the next, we will examine the many subtle ways in which witchcraft seeks to control and influence every aspect of the daily lives of Christians.

A WORK OF THE FLESH

First, we need to understand that witchcraft is primarily a work of the flesh:

> *Now the works of the flesh are evident, which are: adultery, fornication, uncleanness, lewdness, idolatry, sorcery, hatred, contentions, jealousies, outbursts of wrath, selfish ambitions, dissensions, heresies, envy, murders, drunkenness, revelries, and the like.* (Galatians 5:19–21)

Notice that Paul includes idolatry and sorcery in this list. In a number of Bible versions, the word *"sorcery"* is translated as "witchcraft." But, as I pointed out earlier, witchcraft, sorcery, and divination are three aspects of the same dark power. Witchcraft and sorcery are expressions of the carnal nature of man. And, as we observed earlier, an individual operating under the carnal nature desires to control, or have dominion, over other people to get them to do what that individual wants. Such a desire never comes from God. It is an expression of man's fallen nature.

Second, very frequently, we see that a manifestation of witchcraft is not only the work of the flesh but also the work of an evil spirit—of a demon that has entered a person who has indulged in the flesh. Anyone may struggle with lust simply as an expression of man's fallen nature. But if a person regularly and repeatedly indulges in lust in some form, they will almost always end up a slave to a demon of lust. The same can be true of hatred, fear, or any of a number of strong emotions. Basically, these are all natural inclinations of our fallen nature. But when we yield to them, or cater to them, almost invariably, a demonic element enters the situation. This is a pattern for one of the ways Satan seeks to control people.

THE "TIGER"

There are three key words in relation to the presence and operation of witchcraft: (1) *manipulation*, (2) *intimidation*, and (3) *domination*. The end goal is always the third one—domination, or control. Thus, there are two different routes to control: one is by manipulation and the other is by intimidation.

It will be helpful for us to look at some examples of manipulation and intimidation. I want you to visualize a tiger that has one goal—to control you. Whether you encounter controlling behavior in yourself or in others, remember this tiger. Even though you might meet a "tiger" in different circumstances than what I describe here, you will recognize it for what it is. Helping you see the enemy's attempt to control is my objective, so you can identify the tiger of manipulation when it is ready to pounce.

MANEUVERING FOR WHAT WE WANT

Based on Psalm 58, it seems that having a manipulative spirit can begin at birth:

The wicked are estranged from the womb; they go astray as soon as they are born, speaking lies. (verse 3)

Let me give you a very simple example of this. A baby is in its crib, and its diaper is wet, so it cries out of discomfort. Along comes Mommy, who picks it up, changes its diaper, and then gives it a soothing cuddle. After several instances of this, whenever the baby wants to be cuddled, it cries, even though its diaper is not wet. What is that? Manipulation. You don't have to be grown up to practice that kind of controlling behavior!

APPEALING TO THE FLESH

We now turn to a few less "innocent" examples from contemporary culture. First, consider the field of advertising. Much of advertising can be ethical and honest, and it serves a useful purpose. However, in advertising, there is also a great amount of concealed witchcraft, in that it appeals very subtly to people's pride and covetousness. I have talked with people in the advertising world, and you might be amazed at the psychological expertise that goes into developing advertising campaigns. What are the purposes of this manipulation? It seems to me there are two goals: (1) to make you want what you don't need, and (2) to convince you to buy what you can't afford. Those are often the major motivations of advertising today.

What does this manipulation produce? Among other things, it can lead to addictions. Years ago, one famous advertisement for cigarettes featured a beautiful mountain scene with a rugged man in a cowboy hat on a majestic horse. It didn't even need a caption. What was it saying to people? "Marlboro. Why don't you have a smoke?"

I recall walking down a street in a city in England and seeing an advertisement with a healthy, happy-looking man holding a tankard of beer. Once more, the ad didn't even have to have a caption. One look at the man and you would think, "I'd like a beer."

There is another addiction that isn't as commonly talked about, but it is also driven through advertising. It is shopping. Shopping is an addiction for many people. Once, I happened to be driving in our car behind a lady from our church, and she had a bumper sticker that read, "I was born to shop!" I thought to myself, "What a confession from a born-again Christian!" Although we may joke about this, shopping can actually be a very destructive addiction.

CONTROLLING A FAMILY MEMBER

Another area of control is husband-wife relationships. Many husbands and wives are frequently taken over by witchcraft. Generally speaking (although not always), a man will use intimidation and a woman will respond by using manipulation. This may be a little hard to accept, but I have learned by observation that manipulation more frequently affects women than men. On the other hand, when it does take over a man, it makes him a monster. It is incredibly evil and hard to deal with.

INTIMIDATION

One way a man might control his wife through intimidation is by jealous statements or outbursts. With one couple I know, the man has controlled his wife in this way for at least forty years. If she steps outside the boundaries he has decreed for her, he becomes so insanely jealous that she lives in fear of what he might do.

Another male tactic is sulking. I know of a family very close to me who had to deal with this. In fact, it was my own family when I was growing up! My father was a good man, and he was a successful officer in the British army. But if certain things didn't please him, he would go into a sulk, and for forty-eight hours, he wouldn't speak. If you brought him a cup of tea, he wouldn't even thank you. Well, no woman wants to endure that kind of treatment. Some women will do almost anything to avoid it. What is the undiagnosed motive in his heart? Control. To get his way, one way or another.

In another illustration, suppose the husband is an angry man, full of rage. He shouts at his wife and children in order to get what he wants.

His family members cringe in fear and say, "Let's do everything we can to prevent that from happening again. Let him have his way. Let him do whatever he wants." What was his motivation? Control. And that is what he has achieved.

MANIPULATION

Now let's look at the other side. A wife won't normally use intimidation—although there are exceptions. Once, a man in our fellowship came and asked my first wife, Lydia, and me for help with his wife. We drove him back to his home, and his wife was standing in the doorway with a butcher's knife in her hand! But that is not a common scenario. Normally, the woman will take the route of manipulation, which can be manifested in various forms, including emotional breakdowns. Such manipulation is not necessarily planned. It can be influenced by the unseen, supernatural realm.

For instance, years ago, I knew a wonderful Christian family. They were all committed believers, but the wife had a background in the occult. (In those days, we didn't know how to deal with that spiritual issue.) She also had very strong ideas about how the house should be run. If things didn't go her way, she would get a migraine headache, which put her in real agony. The message would be passed along from one family member to another: "Mother's got a migraine. Don't make a noise. Tiptoe around, and don't disturb her." What was that? Manipulation. It wasn't planned. It wasn't conscious. But its origin was in the supernatural occult realm.

Another way wives sometimes manipulate their husbands is by guilt. Suppose a husband has been callous and unkind, and he doesn't deal with his failure to relate properly. But then, every time the wife wants her way, she will gently insinuate and remind him of the way he mistreated her. What is the result? The husband feels guilty and does what she wants. Making people feel guilty is one of the most effective methods of manipulation.

In my view, the Holy Spirit never makes a person feel guilty. Rather, the Holy Spirit *convicts* of sin. (See John 16:8.) So, if you are struggling with guilt, it is not from the Holy Spirit.

WITHHOLDING AFFECTION

There is another very serious way in which wives manipulate husbands and husbands manipulate wives, and that is by withholding affection in the sexual relationship. This practice is explicitly forbidden in Scripture:

> Let the husband render to his wife the affection due her [this includes the sexual relationship], and likewise also the wife to her husband. The wife does not have authority over her own body, but the husband does. And likewise the husband does not have authority over his own body, but the wife does. Do not deprive one another except with consent for a time, that you may give yourselves to fasting and prayer; and come together again so that Satan does not tempt you because of your lack of self-control.
> (1 Corinthians 7:3–5)

I have had to minister to couples along these lines. A wife does not have the right to refuse sexual relations to her husband, nor does a husband have the right to refuse sexual relations to his wife. However, I want to add this word of caution: I am talking about what I would call normal, healthy sex. I am not suggesting women should be subjected to perverse and filthy experiences in the name of sex. I hope I have made myself clear. I have deep compassion for what some women are dragged through in the name of the sexual relationship in marriage.

GENERATIONAL WITCHCRAFT

Let's look at some further expressions of witchcraft. In many cases, witchcraft is inherited by women through the female line, from generation to generation. Many female babies are born with a spirit of witchcraft in them. I don't want to offend anyone, but one area of the world where I have noticed this type of control is in the Deep South, in places like Alabama, Mississippi, Georgia, Louisiana, and so on. There is a tradition of "the Southern lady" who tends to be manipulative. It passes from one generation to another. My wife and I once tried to minister to a pastor's wife who had that background. When we came face-to-face with the root of her problem, it was almost a physical battle to deal with the deep-seated spirit of manipulation.

If you sense you have inherited this problem, you have to face it and call out to God for deliverance. It will not be an easy deliverance—it will be as if something is being wrenched out of you. I am not saying God cannot do it—He can—but it can be a major conflict.

CHILDREN, TOO

Additionally, children can manipulate their parents. Generally speaking, they do so by rebelliousness expressed in temper tantrums. It is embarrassing for parents, especially in the presence of visitors, if their child throws a temper tantrum—lying on the floor, kicking their legs in the air, and screaming. Rather than deal with this behavior in a firm and authoritative way, parents often try to simply hush the child up or take them out of the room so people won't be embarrassed.

One of our daughters used a different form of parental manipulation as a little girl. When she knew my wife Lydia had guests, she would come into the room and say, "Mama, may I have a cookie?" She knew my wife wouldn't refuse her when the guests were there, whereas normally it wouldn't be the time for eating sweets.

Parents must not let themselves be manipulated by their children. It is the worst thing any parent can do for them because they are starting them out on a bad course in life. When the children grow up and get married, they are going to be a terror to somebody if their parents haven't dealt with their manipulative behavior beforehand.

PARENTAL ISSUES

On the other hand, in what ways do parents manipulate their children? One way is by possessiveness, which I think is a terrible form of manipulation. It cultivates a dependence in children upon one or both parents. I met a man who must have been at least thirty years old who was a minister on the preaching circuit. He said to me, "Ever since I left home at the age of eighteen, no matter where I am in the world, I phone my mother long distance every night." I didn't need to know any more. He was being manipulated. He had been trained in dependence. He would feel guilty if, at any time, he offended his mother.

Another way parents manipulate their children is by exploiting their affection. "If you love Mommy, you'll go down to the store for her." Mothers need to know this is the wrong way to talk to their children. Saying, "If you love Mommy, you will do this or that" is manipulation.

Another form of this type of control is convincing children that your love for them depends on their good behavior. As you look back on your childhood, do you feel as if you had to earn your parents' love by obedience? The love of parents should not be earned—it should be freely given. Every child should feel absolutely secure in the fact that his father and mother love him, even when they misbehave. This doesn't mean the parents should indulge the misbehavior. However, there should never be an issue where the child is left wondering, "Do my parents really love me?"

FACING THE TIGER

Whether we are faced with control coming directly from someone we know or indirectly through advertising, entertainment, or social media, we need to recognize the "tiger" as it gets ready to pounce. What I have tried to emphasize in this chapter are the subtle ways in which we may try to control other people, and in which others may try to control us. This is the "tiger" we must learn to recognize so we can deal effectively with the power and influence witchcraft seeks to exert over our lives and the lives of those around us. We now know the ultimate source of negative control. It comes from the carnal nature of fallen man, which is then often exploited by supernatural, evil forces of witchcraft.

In the next chapter, we will tackle the problem of control, or witchcraft, in the church.

25

WITCHCRAFT IN THE CHURCH

It is unpleasant to accept the fact that witchcraft exists in the church, but it is a reality we must face. I have often stated that the very moment someone becomes a Christian, they have signed up for a war. We are in a war between two spiritual kingdoms—the kingdom of God and the kingdom of Satan.

Witchcraft is the enemy's number-one tactic against God's people. We must understand witchcraft in disguise in the church in order to fight the battle wisely. Revival in the church and the world depends upon our success in this battle—and we have every reason to rejoice that the cause of Christ will prevail!

An entire book could be written on the ways in which witchcraft, especially in the form of manipulation, exercises its control in the church. Therefore, in this chapter, I will offer some common examples.

FUND-RAISING

First, let's take a look at how many church leaders appeal for money. A number of preachers, pastors, and evangelists seem to feel it is necessary to manipulate their supporters in order to raise funds. One technique I have seen is to hold a meeting or banquet for donors, during which someone stands up and announces, "There are five people here tonight who are going to give five thousand dollars each to this ministry!" One after another, four people rather sheepishly stand up. Everybody else is wondering, "Am I the fifth?" Eventually, some poor sap stands up and pledges five thousand dollars. But what motivated him? Guilt. Remember, God never motivates by guilt. This scenario is something I have seen over and over again in various parts of the world.

Another way preachers can use manipulation to obtain donations is by giving harrowing descriptions of all the tragic situations they have seen. It is not difficult to manipulate people's emotions if you tell them stories of tremendous suffering. I believe it is right to tell the truth about the situations of the sick, poor, and suffering in our world. I believe it is right to let people know of their need for help. However, I also believe it is totally wrong to cause people to give money out of a sense of guilt. It is a satanic substitute for the proper approach.

Another very common method in the United States, especially among television evangelists, is to make promises, such as "You will receive your healing if you send five hundred dollars to this ministry!" or, "If you want your family to be blessed, send a generous offering, and I will pray for God's blessing on your family." That is manipulation. Some of these people may have been misled, but many of them are liars! And we know where liars end up. It is always important to bear that in mind.

FEAR AND THREATS

Control through fear and threats is another technique. The pastor says, "If you leave this church, you will never prosper." I tell an anecdote in my book *Blessing or Curse* about a pastor who actually spoke those words to a church member. The person to whom he said it was a businessman, and that man did not prosper for the next ten years. His pastor had actually put a curse on him. That is a form of witchcraft.

I have also seen, time and again, the demand for unquestioning loyalty to a pastor or ministry. "I am your pastor, and you have to obey me. If you don't obey what I say, you are disobeying God." That is an out-and-out lie! Sadly, this is very common.

Another way of manipulating unsuspecting church members is to get them into a "covenant." I have been associated with a number of churches that started by drawing up a written covenant everybody in the church had to sign, promising they would never "break fellowship," never separate, and always be accountable to one another. I cannot think of a single church that participated in such a covenant that survived. I believe such covenants are unscriptural because all Christians are already united by a covenant with God through the blood of Jesus. We do not have to make a "special" covenant. This is a satanic substitute.

What normally happens (and I have personally been through this) is that you eventually realize, "I just don't belong here. I don't agree with these people or believe the way they do. I don't think they are totally ethical. I am leaving." And then, do you know what you get called when you leave? A covenant-breaker. How many people want to be called a covenant-breaker? It is all part of gross manipulation.

What I have just described are two marks of a cult: the demand for unquestioning loyalty and the labeling of persons as covenant-breakers if they ever decide to separate from the group. Wherever you encounter those two characteristics, you have encountered a cult. There are many Christian cults, so if you suspect you are entangled in one of them, I would say this to you: have the courage to get out. Don't remain a slave for the rest of your life. Don't be manipulated by guilt or fear.

ABUSING SPIRITUAL GIFTS

Unfortunately, sometimes we see manipulation emerge in the use of spiritual operations, such as the gift of interpretation following an utterance in tongues. I was involved for many years in the Pentecostal movement, and I think I can say I have just about seen it all. For example, I remember when the Pentecostal movement in Britain was in its fledgling beginnings. There would be a humble, struggling pastor with a congregation of about fifty. Often, there would be two or three strong women in that congregation who felt they knew exactly what the pastor should do. If he didn't do what they recommended, one of them would receive a "tongue" and the other would receive an "interpretation." They would use these supposed manifestations of spiritual gifts as a means to "straighten him out." Do you know what that was? It was manipulation, and it had nothing to do with the Holy Spirit or the genuine gifts of tongues and interpretation.

Even prayer can be used as a controlling influence on people. This may shock you, but I don't believe we should ever try to control anybody by prayer. I was once in a situation like that involving a young man who was sick. Certain ladies who respected my ministry were convinced I was the one to pray for this young man. Well, I prayed about it, but I didn't feel I was the one to minister to him. I later heard they were trying to compel me, by their prayers, to go and pray for this young man. The more I learned about that situation, the more I was certain their "leading" didn't come from God. I think they were good ladies—but they were misguided.

CONTROLLING THROUGH THE SUBCONSCIOUS

For a while, a particular idea caught on in the United States that was very evil: if you really wanted someone you knew to do what you felt was the right thing, you got up early in the morning, went to where they were sleeping, and spoke to their subconscious mind. It was a movement led by a certain woman whom I could name but won't. By speaking to people's subconscious minds, you would try to get them to think, say, and do what you believed they should be thinking, saying, and doing. That is nothing less than witchcraft.

"CHARISMATIC FORTUNE-TELLING" AND FLATTERY

Then, there is what I call "charismatic fortune-telling." In Ezekiel 12:24, the Lord is condemning the sins that led to the destruction of Jerusalem, and He says,

For no more shall there be any false vision or flattering divination within the house of Israel.

The church today is filled with "false visions and flattering divination." For the purposes of this chapter, let me strongly warn you against one of these sins—flattery. Proverbs 29:5 says,

A man who flatters his neighbor spreads a net for his feet.

Many times, people will seek to ensnare us by flattery, especially by flattering "prophecies" in which someone says, for example, "You're going to be a real apostle," or "God has called you to be a prophet," or "You're going to pastor a large congregation." What does that appeal to? Pride.

Make no mistake, I believe in prophecy. Many important events in my life have been predicted by prophecy and then fulfilled. I believe in the gifts of a word of wisdom and a word of knowledge. But I also believe there is a satanic counterfeit for each one of those genuine spiritual gifts.

Let me suggest one way to identify the counterfeit. I quote the words of Jesus in John 16:14, where He is speaking about the Holy Spirit:

He will glorify Me, for He will take of what is Mine and declare it to you.

One of the supreme ministries of the Holy Spirit is to glorify Jesus. Wherever glory is being given to someone other than God and Jesus, you can question whether it is from the Holy Spirit. As soon as a human personality is put front and center and lifted up, your attention is directed away from God and toward them: "He's the man with the answers." "He's the man you can go to." "She'll give you the true word of knowledge." Basically, it is very unlikely that such statements come from the Holy Spirit because He does not glorify people—He glorifies God the Son, Jesus Christ.

The Holy Spirit is an encourager, and He will speak words of encouragement to us. However, again, these words will bring glorify to Jesus. I have received words of encouragement many times, and I thank God for these words. But none of them glorified Derek Prince. Just keep an eye on who is in the limelight and who is being lifted up.

Do you know how to invite the presence of the Holy Spirit? It is very simple. Lift up Jesus. The more you lift up Jesus, the happier the Holy Spirit is. You don't have to force Him to come. You don't have to "work Him up." The Holy Spirit is ready to come. He will come when you speak about Jesus and the cross.

Whenever you put a man or woman, a movement, an organization, or even an experience in the place of Jesus, you are on dangerous ground. For example, many Pentecostals have gone astray through glorifying the baptism in the Holy Spirit. They have put the baptism in the place of Jesus.

I have told my Pentecostal brothers many times, "Listen, it is not as important to preach *about* the power of the Holy Spirit. What matters is to preach *in* the power of the Holy Spirit."

SEXUAL SEDUCTION

Regarding witchcraft in the church, there is another problem that is extremely serious, and I must mention it: sexual seduction. I believe there is a tremendous amount of this occurring in the church today. Both males and females can be victimized by it. For men in leadership, it can happen through counseling women—especially distressed women, neglected women, or women who are starved for affection. It may begin with a very innocent motivation, but it can end up in sexual immorality. I believe all of us who are in ministry need to protect ourselves. Personally, I never counsel a woman alone.

During the period when I was a widower, if I was asked to counsel a woman, I would always ask a mature Christian woman to sit in on the session. I never exposed myself to that temptation. When I remarried, my wife would sit in on such sessions. I would advise any Christian man in ministry to follow this practice. The same applies for a woman who may be in a position to minister to men.

Unfortunately, women are often seduced by males in positions of spiritual authority. A case occurred in a very large church in the southeastern United States that had many thousands of members. It was discovered that the male leaders were teaching the women who served under them that when these women reached a certain degree of spiritual growth, it was a good thing to have a sexual relationship with them. It was considered a mark of maturity. This led to the destruction of many women, until one woman had the guts to blow the whistle on the situation. The story was reported in major newspapers throughout the United States.

In a different situation, my wife Ruth and I had a dear Christian friend whom I had known for probably twenty years. He was a mature pastor with over forty years in the ministry. This man had established a large, successful church with many satellite churches and had trained up a whole generation of young leaders. One day, a friend phoned us and said, "Do you have your seat belt fastened? Because I have to tell you something that will shock you." He told us that, on a certain day, this minister had prayed with his wife as usual in the morning, gone to his church office, left divorce papers for his wife on his desk, walked out, locked the door, gotten into his car, and promptly disappeared. Later, it turned out he had set a date to marry another woman.

When Ruth and I heard this, we went to prayer, and God intervened in a marvelous way. The other woman decided to return to her family. But the shock and damage to that congregation, and to the entire city, was tragic. If there was ever a man you would have considered mature, stable, and dependable, it was that man. (I have to say *nobody* is exempt from such temptations.) As I meditated on this situation, a passage came to me from Proverbs 7. We will look at just the last part of the chapter, which speaks about the prostitute and her victim:

> *With her enticing speech she caused him to yield, with her flattering lips she seduced him.*   (verse 21)

Did you notice the word *"flattering"*?

> *Immediately he went after her, as an ox goes to the slaughter, or as a fool to the correction of the stocks, till an arrow struck his liver. As a bird hastens to the snare, he did not know it would cost his life. Now therefore, listen to me, my children; pay attention to the words of my mouth: Do not let your heart turn aside to her ways, do not stray into her paths; for she has cast down many wounded, and all who were slain by her were strong men.*   (Proverbs 7:22–26)

One very conspicuous feature of witchcraft is that it goes after strong men. Its number-one target is strong leadership. Unfortunately, it is often successful.

WHAT CAN WE DO?

You may be thinking, "Brother Prince, you have told us everything that can go wrong. Please tell us what we can do that is right." I could give a lengthy answer, but let me simply mention 2 Corinthians 1:12, in which Paul is speaking about himself and his ministry:

> *For our boasting is this: the testimony of our conscience that we con-*
> *ducted ourselves in the world in simplicity and godly sincerity, not with*
> *fleshly wisdom but by the grace of God, and more abundantly toward*
> *you.*

I suggest that the remedy is *"simplicity and godly sincerity."* In the margin of my Bible is a comment on the word *"simplicity."* It is the opposite of duplicity. In other words, let us be absolutely open and frank, holding no hidden personal agendas, no concealed motives, and no secret relationships. Let us *"walk in the light as He is in the light"* (1 John 1:7).

Taking the right action sometimes requires confrontation. I happen to know, being British to the core, that there is one activity British people like to avoid, and that is confrontation. People from other nations are not like that. I have come to see it is a form of cowardice to avoid confrontation. Let me read just two verses from Proverbs in this regard. (Please notice how many times I have quoted verses from Proverbs. The wisdom of Proverbs is really what we need in these days.) Here is Proverbs 27:5:

> *Open rebuke is better than love carefully concealed.*

This means it is better to challenge a person openly than to love them secretly. Then, in Proverbs 28:23, we read,

> *He who rebukes a man will find more favor afterward than he who*
> *flatters with the tongue.*

Note the use of the word *flattery* again. If there is something wrong in the life of someone who is close to you—maybe a behavior that offends you or offends the church—don't try to deal with it by going through the back door and using flattery. Go through the front door. Challenge them openly.

A REDEMPTIVE EXAMPLE

Let me give you an example from Paul's ministry of challenging someone openly. The apostle wrote in Galatians 2:11:

Now when Peter had come to Antioch, I withstood him to his face, because he was to be blamed.

Peter was the leader of the apostles, so confronting him took some guts on Paul's part.

For before certain men came from James, he would eat with the Gentiles; but when they came, he withdrew and separated himself, fearing those who were of the circumcision. (verse 12)

Out of fear of *"certain men"* who were still following the law of Moses, Peter withdrew from eating with newly converted Gentile Christians. For this infraction, Paul "called Peter out."

And the rest of the Jews also played the hypocrite with him.... (verse 13)

Notice the frankness of Paul's language. He called them "hypocrites."

...so that even Barnabas was carried away with their hypocrisy. But when I saw that they were not straightforward about the truth of the gospel, I said to Peter before them all, "If you, being a Jew, live in the manner of Gentiles and not as the Jews, why do you compel Gentiles to live as Jews?" (verses 13–14)

This is an example of the right way to deal with a very difficult situation. Paul confronted Peter publicly because Peter was, in effect, publicly supporting an erroneous practice that needed to be corrected. Again, for Paul to confront Peter publicly took some courage, because Paul was junior to Peter. Peter was the great apostle, the leader chosen by Jesus. But in Antioch, motivated by fear, Peter did something he shouldn't have. If this happened today, do you know what most church people would do? They would start an anti-Peter movement. They would go behind his back, gather a group of people together, and say, "Have you seen what Peter is doing? He's being a hypocrite!"

If Paul had done that, he would have been engaging in what I call "church politics," which are carnal and inappropriate. We must learn to be open and frank with one another—in humble love, not in bitterness or with a haughty attitude. We need to follow Paul's example, which can produce redemptive results for everyone involved.

26

A PRAYER OF DELIVERANCE

If what I have said concerning witchcraft does not apply to you, then you don't have to take any further action regarding it. But if you sense that some or even all of it does apply to you, I want to lead you in steps toward freedom.

ADDRESSING THE ISSUES

If you are a man, perhaps you have been domineering, using your strength and your temper to inflict your will upon your wife and children. If you are a woman, perhaps you have been manipulative and gone behind your husband's back or used inappropriate tactics to get him to do what you want. If you are a parent, perhaps you have tried to manipulate your children into being dependent upon you. Perhaps, as a church member, you have engaged in church politics to gain influence or control others.

Based on the last few chapters, if you acknowledge to yourself, "I have a problem with a form of witchcraft in my life. What Derek has described in some way applies to me," then there are two possible responses. First, if you are involved in the use of witchcraft in any way, no matter how subtle, in order to control others—then repent and renounce it. If, on the other hand, some form of witchcraft is being used against you—refuse and reject it.

You may also find yourself in both categories. You may be using witch-craft against someone at the same time someone else is using it against you. Either way, at the end of this chapter, you will have an opportunity to pray a prayer for freedom. If you truly want to be free, you can experience the release you seek, if you will humble yourself and meet God's conditions.

Additionally, if you are a woman for whom witchcraft may be an inherited power that has dominated your family from generation to generation, you may also have to receive special counseling. Often, the best person for a woman to go to for help first in this circumstance is her husband. That idea may not appeal to you, but your husband is the spiritual priest of your family and he can minister to you in such a situation. To illustrate this truth, let me tell you about an incident that happened some years ago.

SET FREE

I was preaching on deliverance at an Episcopal church, and a woman at the back of the room became very angry at what I was saying. She got up and started to leave the church, dragging her husband with her. But on her way out, God convicted her, and they turned around and came back into the meeting. When the meeting ended, she came up by herself to talk to me. Before she began to tell me her problem, God gave me the wisdom to ask her, "Where is your husband?" She answered, "He's in the back," as though she were rather reluctant to acknowledge his presence.

I told her, "Call your husband forward and then you can tell me your problem." So she did. While she was recounting her situation, she was continually saying, "God told me this" and "God told me that." After a while, I said, "You know, it must be terrible to live with you, because disagreeing with you is like disagreeing with Almighty God."

For the first time, her husband smiled! At last somebody had understood his problem! Then I said to her, "Now, listen. I'm not the one to pray for you to be delivered. Your husband is your priest and you should ask him to pray for you." She looked at me and then she looked at him—and there was a long silence. Then, rather reluctantly, she asked her husband, "Will you pray for me?" The moment she said those words, she started to be delivered. Why? Because she had begun to meet God's condition, and she had humbled herself.

My word to wives is that they not bypass their husbands when seeking deliverance from witchcraft or for other spiritual needs. If a husband is a believer with some understanding of the things of God, his wife should go to him first. Then, the two of them may need to receive further counseling together.

EXPELLING DEMONS

The Bible says that *"whoever calls on the name of the LORD shall be saved* [or delivered]" (Romans 10:13). So, if you will call on the name of the Lord and meet His conditions, you will be delivered. I will soon lead you in a simple prayer for calling on the name of the Lord. When you have prayed the prayer and said amen, simply stop praying. Why? Because you don't receive deliverance by praying. You receive deliverance by expelling evil spirits. I like the Weymouth translation of Mark 16:17, which says,

> And signs shall attend those who believe, even such as these. By making use of my name they shall expel demons.

How do we deal with demons? We expel them. As long as we are praying nice, religious prayers or even speaking in tongues, we may be blocking the way for the demons to leave. So, say your prayer and then expel! Breathe out the evil spirit. A spirit is a breath. The terms *spirit* and *breath* are the same word in Greek. Most spirits come out through the mouth. Not all, but most. That is why we need to breathe out to expel them.

This is where your pride could get in your way. You might say to yourself, "I feel stupid praying about witchcraft. It can't really be a modern-day problem." Well, you have to choose between two things: your dignity or your deliverance. Here is my advice: let your dignity go and receive your deliverance. After you have been delivered, your dignity will come back. You won't lose it.

Are you ready? Are you prepared to take strong action against your enemy and get rid of him? If so, please pray the following prayer and then take action. Say these words out loud, speaking them to Jesus:

Lord Jesus Christ, I believe You are the Son of God and You died on the cross for my sins and rose again from the dead. I now repent of all my sins and turn from them. I renounce and reject all of them.

In particular, I renounce and reject the sin of witchcraft. I repent of trying to control other people to get them to do what I want. I confess this as a sin and recognize there may be a spirit of witchcraft in my life that causes me to commit this sin. If that is so, I ask for Your forgiveness and I receive it now by faith. I take my stand against witchcraft. I break its hold over my life. I renounce it and I expel it, in the name of Jesus.

Now, breathe out. Expel the evil spirit and let it go. Once it is gone, rejoice in the freedom Christ has given you!

PART SIX:
GETTING DESPERATE

27

WHEN GOD INTERVENES

In the previous sections, we examined three major "stones in the road," or hindrances, to an outpouring of revival: pride, legalism, and witchcraft. All three of these manifestations of our fallen human nature originate in our desire to live independently of God.

Because of that deep-seated independence, God often has to bring us to the end of our own efforts. We have to come to a place of absolute dependence upon Him before He will intervene in our circumstances. In that place of dependence, we realize that our only hope is in Him. It is His mercy that allows us to come to a place of *desperation.*

The theme of desperation may not be popular or appealing to us. But if we understand that it is an expression of God's mercy—His gracious preparation for an outpouring of His Spirit—then it can become a message of hope for us.

THE RETURN OF THE MESSIAH

Many years ago, I was teaching a series of messages from the book of Zechariah about what lies ahead for Israel. In one particular session, I came to Zechariah 14:1–3, which is a prophetic picture of the return of the Messiah in glory. It is the climax of Israel's history, and Christian history as well. Before this event can take place, however, there are numerous difficulties that the people of Israel will have to go through.

Zechariah paints a vivid picture of these troubles, addressing these words to Jerusalem:

> *Behold, the day of the* LORD *is coming, and your spoil* [plunder] *will be divided in your midst. For I will gather all the nations to battle against Jerusalem; the city shall be taken, the houses rifled, and the women ravished. Half of the city shall go into captivity, but the remnant of the people shall not be cut off from the city. Then the* LORD *will go forth and fight against those nations, as He fights in the day of battle. And in that day His feet will stand on the Mount of Olives.*
>
> (Zechariah 14:1–4)

Let us ask ourselves a question here: When Jesus went up to heaven, from what exact location did He leave? He left from the Mount of Olives. Two angels told the disciples, "*This same Jesus, who was taken up from you into heaven, will so come in like manner as you saw Him go into heaven*" (Acts 1:11). Jesus went from the Mount of Olives in the clouds. He is coming back in the clouds—and His feet are going to stand on the Mount of Olives.

When this happens, there is going to be a great earthquake, and the mountain is going to be divided in two, with half going north and half going south. I spent the last year of my military service in a British hospital on the Mount of Olives at a point that, I believe, is the exact spot where the mountain will be divided. We know it is an earthquake area, because there was an earthquake there in 1923 that so severely damaged one of the towers of the hospital building that nobody is allowed to enter it. For me, this is a very striking picture—one that I can see in my mind's eye.

HOPING IN GOD

While I was preaching this message from Zechariah, I was having a silent conversation with the Lord. This often happens to me. I was asking God, "If You intended in the beginning to intervene on behalf of the Jewish people and the city of Jerusalem, why did You let half the city go into captivity, with the houses plundered and the women ravished? Why wouldn't You intervene before all that happened?"

Here is the answer that came to me—and it applies to us today as we cry out to God. It is His response to why He has not yet sent the revival for which we are yearning: *The Lord will not intervene until His people have reached a moment of total desperation.* When we come to the point where we know there is absolutely no other hope and no other source of help but God alone—then He will intervene. Getting desperate is God's requirement.

At that meeting, I then said something that surprised even me: "This is what salvation is: Salvation is taking advantage of the only hope you have of escaping from hell—escaping something so terrible that the human mind cannot even comprehend it. There is no other way of escape but to turn to Jesus who died on your behalf. If you don't take that way of escape, then you're lost. I believe someone needs to make that decision tonight."

A young woman immediately came forward, stood right in front of me, and gave her heart to the Lord. Two other men followed soon after. Not many people talk about hell today, but hell is very real, and it is very close. For some people, it will be a matter of closing their eyes in death and finding themselves in hell. We must realize how urgent, even desperate, it is for people to be saved and to escape hell.

By the mercy of the Holy Spirit, these three people who came forward had suddenly found themselves at a point of desperation. This is the principle we will discuss next as it relates to the overall theme of revival. God will move and bring revival to us only when we have come to the moment of desperation.

A CRY FOR MERCY

Why does God wait for us to become desperate? In connection with that question, let's look at a passage from the book of Isaiah:

Therefore the LORD will wait, that He may be gracious to you; and therefore He will be exalted, that He may have mercy on you.
(Isaiah 30:18)

The Lord is waiting until He can have mercy on us. He is waiting until we meet the conditions.

For the LORD *is a God of justice; blessed are all those who wait for Him. For the people [Israel] shall dwell in Zion at Jerusalem; you shall weep no more. He will be very gracious to you at the sound of your cry; when He hears it, He will answer you.* (verses 18–19)

What is the Lord waiting for? The sound of our cry. The *New International Version* reads, "*How gracious He will be when you cry for help!*" (NIV84). The Hebrew word translated "*cry*," *sa-akar*, means a *desperate* call for help. It is the shout of a man who is drowning. As he goes down for the third time, he cries out, "Help!" God is waiting for His people to come to that point—when we are going down for the third time.

The way God interacts with Israel as a nation is a pattern for the way He deals with other nations and with us. There are countless lessons for us to learn from God's encounters with Israel. We have an amazing example of His methods in Deuteronomy 32. Before Israel ever entered the land of Canaan, Moses told them what would happen to them. He predicted that despite all that God had done for them, they would soon become unfaithful to Him. They would turn to idolatry and ultimately be driven out of the land, spending many years in exile. All of this was revealed to Israel before they ever went into Canaan. Then, as they were gathered on the east side of the Jordan, just before they were about to go into the Promised Land, God gave Moses these terrible words:

I will heap disasters on them; I will spend My arrows on them. They shall be wasted with hunger, devoured by pestilence and bitter destruction; I will also send against them the teeth of beasts, with the poison of serpents of the dust. The sword shall destroy outside; there shall be terror within for the young man and virgin, the nursing child with the man of gray hairs. I would have said, "I will dash them in pieces, I will make the memory of them to cease from among men," [note the following] had I not feared the wrath of the enemy, lest their adversaries should misunderstand, lest they should say, 'Our hand is high; and it is not the LORD *who has done all this.'"* (Deuteronomy 32:23–27)

God gives His reason for turning from judgment of Israel to intervening for Israel. Essentially, He says, "For the honor of My name, I'm going to intervene. Otherwise, your enemies will think that they are the ones who brought all this disaster upon you."

BEYOND OUR POWER

Further along in the same chapter, we read that this is all part of the same vision:

> For the LORD will judge His people and have compassion on His servants, when He sees that their power is gone, and there is no one remaining, bond or free. He will say: "Where are their gods, the rock in which they sought refuge? Who ate the fat of their sacrifices, and drank the wine of their drink offering? Let them rise and help you, and be your refuge." (Deuteronomy 32:36–38)

Do you recognize the same principle? God will not intervene until *"He sees that their power is gone"*—that the personal strength and power of His people have been used up.

Then, God gives this powerful declaration of His sovereignty:

> Now see that I, even I, am He, and there is no God besides Me; I kill and I make alive; I wound and I heal; nor is there any who can deliver from My hand. (verse 39)

We must come to see the total omnipotence and sovereignty of God— and our total need of His mercy. In reality, there is no other hope for any individual, church, or nation but in the mercy of God.

WHERE IS JUSTICE?

In a triumphant conclusion, God says He will avenge those who have persecuted His people. (And that is a very large number of people.) In Deuteronomy 32:43, He says,

Rejoice, O Gentiles, with His people [Israel]; for He will avenge the blood of His servants, and render vengeance to His adversaries; He will provide atonement for His land and His people.

There is something in the heart of every one of us that cries out for justice. Too often, we look at the state of the world and we say, "There is no justice. People get away with all sorts of crimes. They mistreat and oppress people." But here is what I want to unequivocally say: "There is justice. Justice is coming. God will avenge His people, and He will avenge all those who have been mistreated and unjustly abused." We need to believe that.

We also need to understand that the wickedness in the world *is* getting worse. Iniquity is going to increase to a degree that we can hardly dare to imagine. We will need to know how to respond to this increase in evil, violence, cruelty, and immorality. Every kind of filthy, vile practice that has been growing in this nation for the last fifty years—and I have witnessed it—is going to continue increasing. It is not going to get better. It is going to get worse.

If you were to say, "Well, Derek, I think you are a pessimist," this would be my response: "No, I am not. I am a realist. There is a difference. I am not a pessimist, because I believe that 'soon and very soon, we are going to see the King.'" I think that is the only realistic source of hope there is.

Humanity has been trying to straighten itself out for thousands of years. Yet its condition today is worse than it has ever been. To my way of thinking, it is totally unpractical and illogical to expect salvation from the human race. However, we can expect to see salvation from God Almighty. All of what we see taking place in the world is heading toward a dramatic conclusion, as we will see in the next chapter.

28

DESPERATE TIMES

I realize that it is disturbing to talk about the difficult times that cause us to feel desperate, as well as the injustices we see around us in the world. As we continue in this vein, however, keep one thought in mind: *we are heading toward God's harvest hour.*

If we are really honest, we will admit that we sometimes secretly wonder, "Why does God seem to be allowing evil people to get away with what they do? Why isn't God doing anything about the triumph of injustice?" Let's look at some Scriptures that will help to address these questions.

THE END OF THE WICKED

In Psalm 92:7, God has something very specific to say about the wicked:

When the wicked spring up like grass, and when all the workers of iniquity flourish, it is that they may be destroyed forever.

This verse foretells the ultimate end of the wicked. God is saying, "I am going to let the harvest ripen." In Genesis 15, the Lord said to Abraham, in essence, "I'm going to give you the land of Canaan—but not for another four hundred years because the iniquity of the Amorites is not yet complete." (See verse 16.)

This is what we must understand: God is waiting for the harvest of iniquity to come to full ripeness. In the earth today, the harvest of salvation and the harvest of iniquity are both ripening—side by side. That is an amazing thought! In the parable of the wheat and the tares, the same sun and the same rain that ripen the wheat ripen the tares. God is going to deal with them both when the harvest comes in. When will that be? Jesus said, *"The harvest is the end of the age"* (Matthew 13:39).

I am impressed by the following words spoken by an angel to the apostle John in Revelation 22:10–12:

> *Do not seal the words of the prophecy of this book, for the time is at hand. He who is unjust, let him be unjust still; he who is filthy, let him be filthy still; he who is righteous, let him be righteous still; he who is holy, let him be holy still.*

Verse 11 contains the words that really impacted me: *"He who is filthy, let him be filthy still; …he who is holy, let him be holy still."* Again, the two harvests are ripening side by side. The next words are:

> *And behold, I am coming quickly, and My reward is with Me, to give every one according to his work.* (verse 12)

THE CROWN AND THE SICKLE

Therefore, in our world today, we are watching two harvests ripen simultaneously, side by side: the harvest of salvation and the harvest of judgment. In Revelation 14, the two harvests are described one after the other. Let's look at a passage from this chapter, beginning with verse 14:

> *Then I looked, and behold, a white cloud, and on the cloud sat One like the Son of Man [Jesus], having on His head a golden crown….*

The crown referred to in this verse is not a royal crown. Rather, it is the crown worn by a victor. In the New Testament, there are two words for "crown." One is the crown of royalty—a diadem. The other is the crown that was the emblem of the victor in the Olympic Games. In our modern-day Olympics, we give the first-place winner a gold medal. But in the New Testament era, they gave a laurel crown. In most places in the New Testament where you read the word *crown*, it refers to the laurel wreath.

On the other hand, the Bible says that when Jesus comes back to earth riding on His white horse, there will be many diadems, or many kingly realms, all under His kingship.

HARVEST OF SALVATION

Continuing in this passage, we read,

> *…and in His hand a sharp sickle. And another angel came out of the temple, crying with a loud voice to Him who sat on the cloud, "Thrust in Your sickle and reap, for the time has come for You to reap, for the harvest of the earth is ripe."*   (Revelation 14:14–15)

In the original Greek, this last phrase indicates "the harvest of the earth is dry." This meant it had to be reaped or else it would be lost. That is the harvest of salvation. We are seeing this harvest being reaped all around the world today. In nations that traditionally had no desire for Jesus, people are crying out for the gospel. This is the harvest hour.

HARVEST OF WICKEDNESS

Then we come to the next harvest, and this is the correct order in which harvests happen in Israel. First, the grain is harvested. Then, the final harvest is the grapes.

> *Then another angel came out of the temple which is in heaven, he also having a sharp sickle. And another angel came out from the altar, who had power over fire, and he cried with a loud cry to him who had the sharp sickle, saying, "Thrust in your sharp sickle and gather the clusters of the vine of the earth, for her grapes are fully ripe."*
> (Revelation 14:17–18)

Please notice that the harvest is not reaped until it is fully ripe.

So the angel thrust his sickle into the earth and gathered the vine of the earth, and threw it into the great winepress of the wrath of God.
(Revelation 14:19)

This is the harvest of wickedness. Do you know what happens in a winepress when the grapes are gathered? They put the grapes in a large stone basin, and people come and trample them underfoot to crush the juice out. That is the picture of the wicked being thrown into the winepress of the wrath of God. They are to be trampled underfoot. The next verse says,

And the winepress was trampled outside the city, and blood came out of the winepress, up to the horses' bridles, for one thousand six hundred furlongs.
(verse 20)

In a marginal note in my Bible, it says this is equivalent to one hundred and eighty-four miles. Now, many people interpret Revelation "symbolically." I would like to ask you, however, to consider this question: "Do you think this is symbolic blood?" Because I don't. I think it is real blood that is being squeezed out in the winepress of the wrath of God.

In the book of Isaiah, we see a remarkable picture of the One who treads the winepress. Isaiah 63:1 begins, *"Who is this who comes from Edom...?"* Edom is the name for the land east of the Jordan. The word also means "red." It was the name originally given to Esau, because he was covered with red hair. Let's look at the context of this statement from Isaiah:

Who is this who comes from Edom, with dyed garments from Bozrah, this One who is glorious in His apparel, traveling in the greatness of His strength?—"I who speak in righteousness, mighty to save." Why is Your apparel red, and Your garments like one who treads in the winepress? "I have trodden the winepress alone, and from the peoples no one was with Me. For I have trodden them in My anger, and trampled

them in My fury; their blood is sprinkled upon My garments, and I
have stained all My robes."   (Isaiah 63:1–3)

All of this is a picture of Jesus judging the wicked. Revelation 19:13
describes Jesus as wearing "*a robe dipped in blood.*"

A DAY OF VENGEANCE

Isaiah 63:4 then introduces this new thought:

For the day of vengeance is in My heart, and the year of My redeemed
has come.

There is going to be vengeance, my dear reader. God is a God of justice. His justice tarries. But it is absolutely sure and complete. I have heard
many sermons and met many preachers, but it is rare to hear ministers
today talk about the judgment of God. Is that not true? Yet it is a very
significant part of the truth of God's Word. Jesus said that when the Holy
Spirit comes, "*He will convict the world of sin, and of righteousness, and of*
judgment" (John 16:8). How will He ever convict the world of judgment if
we never preach about God's judgment?

A UNIVERSAL PROBLEM

The writer of Psalm 73 had a problem that is strikingly similar to the
problem we are facing today. The unrighteous were flourishing on every
hand. They were bribing the courts, making money, and getting away with
crime. Seeing this inequity, the writer was understandably appalled. In
Psalm 73:12, he said,

Behold, these are the ungodly, who are always at ease; they increase in
riches.

This observation seems to generally hold true. For the most part,
it is the ungodly who are rich. The idea that all Christians ought to
be rich is not scriptural. All Christians should have an abundant suf-
ficiency, but the truth is that riches are mainly for the wicked in this
generation.

THE PROPER RESPONSE

Next, we see the psalmist's initial comment regarding the situation he was facing: *"Surely I have cleansed my heart in vain, and washed my hands in innocence"* (Psalm 73:13). He was saying, in effect, "I've been living a righteous life, and what do I have to show for it? Nothing." Then, he continues, *"For all day long I have been plagued, and chastened every morning"* (verse 14). Most likely, you and I could say the same thing: "'All day long I have been plagued, and chastened every morning.' And yet, I have been leading a righteous life. I haven't gone along with the plans of the wicked."

In the next verse, the psalmist continued, *"If I had said, 'I will speak thus,' behold I would have been untrue to the generation of Your children"* (verse 15). This is a reminder for us to never speak despairingly about following the Lord, because by doing so, we could undermine the faith of a child of God.

"When I thought how to understand this, it was too painful for me— until I went into the sanctuary of God; then I understood their end" (verses 16–17). There are some quandaries we can't understand until we go into the sanctuary of God, or into the presence of God. Understanding doesn't come until we hear from the Lord and are instructed by Him directly through the Holy Spirit. This is what God showed the author of Psalm 73:

> *Surely You set them* [the wicked] *in slippery places; You cast them down to destruction. Oh, how they are brought to desolation as in a moment! They are utterly consumed with terrors. As a dream when one awakes, so, LORD, when You awake, You shall despise their image.* (verses 18–20)

God says that the wealthy wicked have been set in *"slippery places."* On the day they die, they will slip immediately into hell without any alternative. God Himself has put them in slippery places.

How does God expect us to respond to all this? You may think Christians should never talk about vengeance. Perhaps that is true in terms of personal vengeance. But the vengeance of God is a different matter entirely. We need to warn people that *God does take vengeance*. The Bible declares this truth very clearly—He is a God of vengeance.

Usually, when I make a statement like that in front of a crowd of people—even in front of believers—they look at me as if they had never heard this before. But what I am telling you is straight from the Bible. If we don't start telling people the hard truth, who else is going to?

29

THAT NONE SHOULD PERISH

Why doesn't Jesus come now and end all the pain in this world? Why do Christians throughout the globe have to go on in the midst of suffering, misery, and mounting iniquity? Once again, we find ourselves asking the inevitable follow-up question: "What is God waiting for?" Part of the answer is found in 2 Peter 3:9:

> *The Lord is not slack concerning His promise, as some count slackness, but is longsuffering toward us, not willing that any should perish but that all should come to repentance.*

I think the phrase *"longsuffering toward us"* is referring to God's elect—His chosen ones. I believe in God's election. I believe He has those whom He has chosen. Do you? (See, for example, Romans 8:33; Titus 1:1.) And I believe that I am one of them.

THE CHOSEN

Some people have a difficult time with the idea that the Jews are a chosen race. Yet Christians are a chosen "race" as well. We would never be Christians if God had not chosen us. Jesus Himself clearly states this truth when He says to His disciples, *"You did not choose Me, but I chose you..."* (John 15:16). Thus, you cannot really understand the Bible unless you understand God's election.

Just to be clear, I am not a Calvinist. I don't believe some people are chosen to be damned and others to be saved. But the Bible does say:

For whom [God] foreknew, He also predestined to be conformed to the image of His Son, that He might be the firstborn among many brethren. Moreover whom He predestined, these He also called; whom He called, these He also justified; and whom He justified, these He also glorified.   (Romans 8:29–30)

So, what is the Lord waiting for? All whom He has chosen for Himself. He is *"not willing that any should perish but that all should come to repentance"* (2 Peter 3:9). He will not bring final judgment to the world until every last one of His own has come in. He will wait with infinite patience. As much as we long for revival, Jesus is tarrying to give us a chance to share the truth of the gospel with the world. He is giving the world a chance to repent and be saved.

I believe there has to be at least one soul saved from each "nation, tribe, people, and tongue." (See Revelation 7:9.) Therefore, I believe there is no more urgent task for the church than to spread the gospel to the nations that have not yet been reached. Jesus will not return until everyone has been reached. He will not come until there is at least one member of every people group to stand before the throne. God the Father will see to this, because it will glorify His Son, whose sacrifice was poured out for the people of every nation on earth.

A DIFFERENT VIEW OF WICKEDNESS

Thus, God is waiting because of His mercy. For this reason, He will tolerate wickedness that would seem to demand His immediate intervention. Eventually, He will indeed judge the wicked. But, for this moment, He is waiting for every last one whom He has chosen to come into His kingdom.

Throughout my many years in ministry, I have marveled at the way God finds the ones whom He has chosen. He goes to the most amazing lengths to find people who nobody else would ever think were worth considering. But they are chosen children of God. God will not take in the "fishing net" until every last chosen one has received salvation.

In light of this truth, we need to develop a different view of wickedness. We have to see past the evil to God's infinite mercy and patience as He waits for those whom He has chosen. Certainly, we must not be passive in this process. We must do something to help reach the unreached. The motto of our ministry is "to reach the unreached and teach the untaught." Let me say that I usually have no doctrinal issues with anybody who is totally committed to that mission. I find I am in perfect harmony with those who are in some way dedicated to "reaching the unreached and teaching the untaught." If I meet someone who has this commitment, after ten minutes has passed, it feels like we have known each other all our lives.

For Ruth and me, this motto has been our purpose for living. We fully believe in Matthew 24:14:

> And this gospel of the kingdom will be preached in all the world as a witness to all the nations, and then the end will come.

This is what God is waiting for. If anybody is delaying the coming of the Lord, it is we who are believers—because we are not preaching the gospel!

GOD'S CHOICE OF ISRAEL

Just as Christians have been chosen by God to be "*a royal priesthood, a holy nation*" (1 Peter 2:9), so Israel was chosen by God as a nation. I have a deep love for the Jewish people. But it was not always that way. In fact, as a young man, I was like most Gentiles. I had a few good Jewish friends during my school and university years. But basically, I always had a sort of unspoken, inner reservation. My thoughts went something like this: "If the Jews suffer so much, there must be something wrong with them."

I would never have been openly anti-Semitic, but there was in my heart, as in the hearts of many people today—even Christians—an unspoken reservation about the Jewish people. There is something about them that the world as a whole does not altogether like. What does that dislike stem from? Could it be the simple fact that God chose them?

Many years ago, I baptized a dear friend in the Sea of Galilee. Strange as it may seem, when he came up out of the waters of baptism, he asked me this question: "Why did God choose the Jews?" Somewhat surprised at the timing of his question, I looked at him and said, "Why did God choose you?" He had no more questions after that. He understood that God's purposes are often a mystery to us. But here is the truth of the matter: if we don't believe in the choice of the Jews, we have undermined our own salvation. Our salvation depends on God choosing us, just as much as the destiny of the Jewish people depends on God choosing them.

JESUS THE MESSIAH

There is an important event that must occur before the return of Jesus as the Jewish Messiah. In the book of Zechariah, God says,

> *And I will pour on the house of David and the inhabitants of Jerusalem the Spirit of grace and supplication; then they will look on Me whom they pierced. Yes, they will mourn for Him as one mourns for his only son, and grieve for Him as one grieves for a firstborn.*
>
> (Zechariah 12:10)

This is one of the most amazing statements in the Bible. It is the Lord who is speaking, and yet He says, *"They will look on Me whom they pierced."* It is perhaps the clearest single self-identification of Jesus as the pierced Messiah. However, no one can know who Jesus is except by revelation, and that revelation comes from the Holy Spirit. (See, for example, Matthew 16:16–17.) Thus, until the Holy Spirit reveals the Messiah to the Jewish people, they will remain remarkably blind to the truth about Jesus.

I have spoken to many Jewish travel guides who have accompanied Christian tours in Israel. They have heard the truth, they have seen people being prayed for, and they have seen people receive healing. Even so, their attitude is, "I would love to believe, but I can't." The Jewish inability to believe the gospel is, to a large extent, a judgment of God. But that judgment is about to be revoked. Interestingly, among the Jewish people today, it is as if God is sneaking up on their blind side. They don't understand what is happening, but the Holy Spirit is beginning to convict them about the truth that Jesus is the Messiah.

SMALL BEGINNINGS

I first went to Jerusalem in 1942, and I was living there in 1948 when the State of Israel was born. At that time, if you spoke to certain Jewish people about Jesus, they would spit in contempt. However, today, there is a very different attitude. I know of a non-Christian professor in The Hebrew University who teaches about religion—especially Christianity. I heard him say, "Some years ago, my students were only interested in the doctrinal aspects of religion. But now they are all interested in the person of Jesus."

The Orthodox Jews would never call Jesus by His right name, nor would they acknowledge that He is Jewish. The Hebrew word for Jesus is *Yeshua*, but most of them removed the last letter and called Him *Yeshu*, indicating that He was a Gentile. In effect, they were saying, "He doesn't belong to us, and we won't give Him a Hebrew name."

That attitude is also changing. At times, Ruth and I have had Jewish people sit and listen to us talk about Jesus for as long as we were willing. Some of our friends—lawyers, engineers, and people of other professions—would come to our home on business. Then, we would visit together, drinking tea or coffee, and they wouldn't leave! We would think to ourselves, "Why don't they go?" Do you know what they were waiting for? They were waiting to hear about what God had done in our lives. The Jews are very down-to-earth people, and when something works, they want it. The problem is, they haven't seen much Christianity that works.

THE POWER OF GOD

I want to share a particular story in this regard. An eminent Jewish engineer helped us plan the construction of our home in Jerusalem. He was assisting the architect with the plans, and one day after the house was nearly complete, he dropped in to see us. His first words were, "I'm very busy—I can only stay ten minutes." But then he said, "I have such a pain in my back."

Ruth said, "Well, my husband has something for back pain." He got very interested. I stated, "As a matter of fact, I do. But it's a little unusual. I get a person to sit down in a chair and I check their legs. If one leg is shorter than the other, it will grow out. When it does, then you know God has touched you." So, he sat down in the chair. As I held his feet, one leg just shot out! He ended up staying half an hour when he had previously said he could only stay ten minutes.

In fact, he came back about two weeks later, and Ruth asked him, "How is your back?" He said, "It's fine, but does your husband have anything for shoulders?" Ruth replied, "As a matter of fact, he does." So I said, "Yes, I have people stand up straight, stretching their arms out in front of them. If one arm is longer than the other, the short arm grows out. When that happens, you know God has touched you."

He was very willing to stand up and stretch out his arms. When he did, one arm was considerably shorter than the other—and it shot out. He was astonished. It was a hot day and he was wearing a short-sleeved shirt, and the hairs on his arm were all standing up! He said, "What's that?" I answered somewhat nonchalantly, "That is the power of God." "Well," he said, "you could have a line in the street outside if you'd do this."

Later on, he said to another friend of ours, "I believe Jesus was the Messiah." That does not necessarily mean he was saved; it was an intellectual change, not a change of heart. However, it was a step along the way for him.

Through encounters like this, the Holy Spirit is, as I said, "sneaking up on the blind side of the Jewish people." Many advances are taking place that can't be explained except for God initiating the work. There is a change coming as Jesus is being revealed to the Jewish people.

THE SPIRIT OF GRACE AND SUPPLICATION

Let us return now to the prophecy of Zechariah. God prophesied that just before the coming of Israel's Messiah, He would *"pour out on the house of David and the inhabitants of Jerusalem the Spirit of grace and supplication"* (Zechariah 12:10). Grace is the supernatural intervention of God beyond our natural ability. When a person makes supplication to God, he or she is asking for mercy.

In other words, God was saying, "I will pour out upon them a Spirit, the Holy Spirit, who will enable them to pray on a level beyond their own understanding. I will enable them to call out for a mercy they could never seek without the help of My Spirit." The Holy Spirit is the *"Spirit of grace and supplication,"* and with Him, *"they will look on Me whom they pierced"* (verse 10). All of this will come to them by the Spirit of God.

The church also needs *"the Spirit of grace and of supplication"* if it is to see revival. If we are going to pray the kind of prayers that really mean something, we are going to need the supernatural enabling of the Holy Spirit. We are at a point of global crisis, and there is only one source of help: the God whom we have too often ignored, neglected, and slighted. However, He still loves each of us, in spite of our indifference toward Him. He is still willing to pour out His Spirit if the conditions are met.

For example, when I was the pastor of a church in Britain during the 1950s, the people were very unresponsive. The trait that characterized the British people at that time was their indifference. They weren't angry, and they didn't persecute Christians. They were just not interested in the gospel. That is the hardest attitude of all to deal with.

In fact, the most difficult eight years of my entire ministry were the years I spent in London. I finally said, "When I finish here, if God ever wants me back, He's going to have to call me very clearly." Then I went to Kenya, where the people were hungry to know about Jesus. I thought, "What a difference!" But the Lord began to speak to me and remind me that He loves Britain for special reasons.

You see, if you look back over the last four hundred years, Britain has been the nation that has most honored the Bible and done the most to bring the gospel to other countries. In the twentieth century, I think America moved into the top position in that regard, yet I don't believe God will forget what has been done by the British. However, Britain, like every other nation, must call out for His mercy. Our cry cannot come from our intellect. It is not going to be just a decision of our will in which we say, "I'll get up every morning at seven o'clock and pray for revival." That is a wonderful decision, but it is going to take more than that. What it will take is described in the next chapter.

30

LIFE BENEATH THE SURFACE

We ended the previous chapter with the conclusion that it is going to take more than a decision of our will to pray to bring forth revival. So, what is it going to take?

As a way of beginning to address this question, I want to share an illustration that involves a unique region found in South Africa and Namibia: Namaqualand. It is an unusual place because for many months, no rain falls. The whole land is dry and arid without any real vegetation. However, when the spring rains fall, this region becomes the most glorious pageant of colorful flowers. Do you know why? The seeds of thousands of flowers are all there below the surface. But it takes the rain to make them germinate.

I believe most of the traditionally Christian nations today are like Namaqualand. They have been very dry and seemingly lifeless. But underneath the surface, there are seeds of gospel truth that have been sown in those nations for hundreds of years. If God were to pour out His Holy Spirit on those dormant seeds, we would be astonished at what would come up. We would see an amazing display of transforming life and beauty. That is my belief, and I hope it will become your belief, too.

WHAT IS OUR PART?

What part do we have to play in the outpouring of the rain of the Holy Spirit? It is essential for us to understand our part because it is the rain of the Spirit that will bring those seeds to life. To answer this question, we can look to Joel, the prophet of the latter-day outpouring of the Holy Spirit. The book of Joel opens with a picture of desolation—the kind of desperate situation we have been discussing in this section of *The Coming Revival*. There were no crops, either in the fields or on the fruit trees. Everything was withered and destroyed. There was no food for the people or their animals. There was no life. But then, we read this in the middle of chapter 2:

> *"Now therefore," says the* LORD, *"turn to Me with all your heart, with fasting, with weeping, and with mourning." So rend your heart, and not your garments. Return to the* LORD *your God, for He is gracious and merciful, slow to anger, and of great kindness; and He relents from doing harm. Who knows if He will turn and relent, and leave a blessing behind Him.* (Joel 2:12–14)

What was required of the people? Getting desperate.

> *And it shall come to pass afterward that I will pour out My Spirit on all flesh; your sons and your daughters shall prophesy, your old men shall dream dreams, your young men shall see visions. And also on My menservants and My maidservants I will pour out My Spirit in those days. And I will show wonders in the heavens and in the earth: blood and fire and pillars of smoke. The sun shall be turned into darkness, and the moon into blood, before the coming of the great and awesome day of the* LORD. *And it shall come to pass that whoever calls on the name of the* LORD *shall be saved.* (Joel 2:28–32)

When Joel is quoted in the New Testament in Acts 2:17, it says, "*in the last days*" rather than "*afterward*," but both are correct. Let's consider the significance of "afterward" for a moment. After what? After God's people have done what He told them to do: turn to Him with all their heart, with fasting, weeping, and mourning. God says that when that happens, He will pour out His Spirit on all flesh.

This passage very clearly describes the end of the age—"*the great and awesome day of the* LORD." Why is it that whoever calls on the name of the Lord in this situation will be saved? Because the Holy Spirit will have been poured out. When the Holy Spirit is poured out, we will see people streaming into God's kingdom.

AN APPEAL FOR PRAYER

At this point in this book, I want to make an appeal to you. When I was pastoring in London in the 1950s, we prayed every week for revival in Britain. Personally, I don't believe those prayers went unheard, even though that was more than half a century ago. I believe this is also true for all the nations where faithful believers have prayed for decades for revival. However, the final answers are going to require the prayer of desperation.

You must come face-to-face with the fact that there is no other hope. Nothing else will do. Nations will be lost unless God intervenes—and God is waiting for the cry of desperation. We cannot work up a state of desperation. It is no use *trying* to be desperate. Only the Holy Spirit can pour out upon you and me the Spirit of grace and supplication.

Here is my appeal, and I want to say it very carefully. I trust you will ask the Holy Spirit for guidance before you respond. I believe God put it in my heart to ask if you would be one of those who would commit themselves, as the Holy Spirit empowers and enables you, to pray the prayer of desperation. Praying in this desperate way will require a recognition that you have come to the end of yourself.

I know of a Christian mother whose grown son, also a Christian, was planning to marry a young Christian woman. But it was obvious to the entire family that it would be a very unsuitable marriage. He was a stubborn young man, so he planned to go ahead with the wedding anyway. As a result, the mother spent hours on her face before the Lord, crying out on behalf of her son.

Her prayers prevailed and the marriage was cancelled. He is now married to a beautiful Christian woman, and they have two lovely children. But this wasn't the only result. Those concentrated times of prayer changed the mother. They not only changed her son and his future but they also transformed her spiritually. She has never been the same. Something happened in her when God brought her to the point of desperation.

Please consider my challenge carefully. I don't want you to make a superficial response to God. However, I am hoping that the Holy Spirit has been speaking to you. I am hoping you have heard the Holy Spirit ask, "Are you willing to let Me make you desperate for revival in your nation? Are you willing to let Me break through in your life, change your priorities, and, if necessary, cause you to fall on your face on the floor, day after day, until you see the rain fall from heaven?"

Prayer like this is a calling for those whom the Holy Spirit leads. It is not for everybody. The cry of desperation is supernatural and is released by the Holy Spirit. Please understand that if you do not feel called to this, it is not because of any shortcoming in yourself. This is a call from the Holy Spirit and is not based on any merit within ourselves. If He does not lay this on your heart, then it is because He has something else for you to do.

Therefore, take a moment now and listen to the Spirit. See if He is asking you, "Will you let Me make you desperate for your nation?" If you believe God may wish to use you in this way, then simply express your willingness to follow Him in this calling with the following prayer:

Father, I stand in awe in Your presence. Thank You for the challenge of Your Word that has come to me. I cry to You for mercy for my nation. God, have mercy on us! In judgment remember mercy. Enable me by Your grace and by the Holy Spirit to experience a breakthrough in prayer—to pray in desperation for an outpouring of the Holy Spirit. I ask You to draw this nation back to You. Father, I pray for You to move by Your Holy Spirit to bring revival to our land—and throughout the earth. In Jesus's name. Amen.

PART SEVEN:

PURIFYING OURSELVES

31

A CULTURE IN CONFUSION

Part six, "Getting Desperate," dealt with a challenging aspect of the Christian life. God, in His wisdom, allows us to go through the painful process of coming to the end of ourselves so we will cry out to Him for help. We saw how reaching that point of desperation—where nothing and no one but God can help us—can actually become a catalyst for revival. It can be an integral part of God's gracious preparation for an outpouring of His Holy Spirit. Isn't this what we are longing for? Isn't this the kind of revival humanity so desperately needs?

THE WORLD IS FALLING APART

As we see this world plummeting faster and faster toward that final point of desperation, we have to answer one more question: "How can we be 'in' the world but not 'of' it? (See John 17:14–15.) Up until about the middle of the twentieth century, most of the West was what might loosely be called a "Christian" society. By this, I mean that the morals and ethics of the Judeo-Christian heritage strongly influenced how the majority of the people lived. Today, however, it is a radically different world. We see a culture that is not only labeled "post-Christian," but one that is becoming increasingly "anti-Christian."

For much of the early part of my life, I lived mainly in Britain. But I have also lived in Kenya, Israel, and the United States. Throughout the course of my ministry, I have travelled extensively on every continent and have ministered in a vast diversity of cultures. My personal perspective, both from Scripture and from the life I have lived, is this: *the world is falling apart.*

Every day, we see evidence in the news media that the situation is out of control. The politicians cannot control it. The scientists cannot control it. The education specialists cannot control it. Even more, the religious leaders cannot control it.

I could take up a number of pages in this book with evidence to prove that the world is falling apart. However, I would prefer to give you my thoughts about how we can face this situation. How does the Bible tell us to live in a world that is falling apart? How can we do more than just survive?

I have had a good life. It hasn't always been easy. Yet, I can say, like the psalmist, "*The lines have fallen to me in pleasant places*" (Psalm 16:6). However, I am deeply concerned for younger people who are just getting started in life. I am concerned for others as well who are already facing difficult decisions in a culture that is falling into chaos. In the next few chapters, I want to offer some perspective and advice.

THE DAYS OF NOAH AND LOT

To begin with, we will briefly consider a few passages of Scripture that, as I see it, deal with the present age. In Luke 17:26–30, Jesus gives us a picture of what it will be like in the last days preceding His return:

> And as it was in the days of Noah, so it will be also in the days of the Son of man: they ate, they drank, they married wives, they were given in marriage, until the day that Noah entered the ark, and the flood came and destroyed them all. Likewise as it was also in the days of Lot: they ate, they drank, they bought, they sold, they planted, they built; but on the day that Lot went out of Sodom it rained fire and brimstone from heaven and destroyed them all. Even so will it be in the day when the Son of Man is revealed.

I believe these verses describe the days in which we are living. In a very quick scriptural survey, I want to give you six attributes of the days of Noah and Lot that are prominent and increasing today. The first four attributes are of the days of Noah, and I believe the first one is the most important:

First, the human race was infiltrated by evil angels from the kingdom of Satan. (This is recorded in Genesis 6:1–3.) Personally, I believe the same is happening to humanity today.

Second, every thought of man's heart was evil. (See Genesis 6:5.)

Third, the earth was filled with violence. (See Genesis 6:11.) Our present times are probably some of the most violent in human history.

Fourth, sexual perversions were rampant. (See Genesis 6:12.) One of the particular expressions of sexual perversion from the days of Lot was blatant homosexuality. (See Genesis 19:4–5.)

When I was growing up, the word *homosexual* was hardly ever mentioned. It was a topic people simply didn't discuss. Everyone knew there were homosexuals in society, but the majority of them chose to stay out of the public eye. Today, homosexuals are some of the most aggressive people in the world. It was the same in the days of Lot.

In the account in Genesis 19, when Lot's two angelic visitors came to Sodom and he urged them to stay in his house, all the men of the city— please take note, *all the men of the city*—gathered around and said, in effect, "Where are the men? Bring them out so we may have sexual relations with them."

A fifth feature of the days of Noah and the days of Lot was materialism. According to Jesus, people were eating, drinking, marrying, giving in marriage, building, planting, buying, and selling. (See Luke 17:26–30.) Please understand that there is nothing wrong with any of those activities. But the men and women of Noah's and Lot's days were so deeply immersed in their lifestyle that they didn't know what was about to come upon them. I believe the same may be true of the majority of professing Christians today. Many are so taken up with materialism that they do not understand the judgments of God which are coming upon this nation and the other nations of the world.

Jesus cites a sixth attribute in Matthew 24. Speaking about the *"birth pains"* (verse 8 NIV), or labor pains, that will introduce a new age when the kingdom of God is established on earth, He says there will be wars: *"For nation will rise against nation, and kingdom against kingdom"* (Matthew 24:7).

Here is an important note: the Greek word translated *"nation"* is *ethnos*, from which we derive the word *ethnic*. I believe ethnic and racial conflict will be one of the great labor pains of this age. It is widespread in Eastern Europe, the Middle East, and Africa, and it is expanding into many other places with unbelievable rapidity. Groups that have been able to live together in comparative peace are now at one another's throats across the earth. Such nations as the United States and Great Britain, which have a great multiplicity of ethnic groups, will continue to see growing racial tensions. At some point, these ethnic and racial tensions will intensify into armed conflict. I think this will be one of the most distinctive characteristics of the age in which we live.

IRREVERSIBLE CORRUPTION

Let's continue our examination of the characteristics of the end times by looking at a passage in 2 Timothy. Paul writes the following words concerning the condition of society in the last days:

> But know this, that in the last days perilous times will come: for men will be lovers of themselves, lovers of money, boasters, proud, blasphemers, disobedient to parents, unthankful, unholy, unloving, unforgiving, slanderers, without self-control, brutal, despisers of good, traitors, headstrong, haughty, lovers of pleasure rather than lovers of God.
>
> (2 Timothy 3:1–4)

The Greek word that is translated as *"perilous"* is used in only one other place in the New Testament, which describes two demon-possessed men coming out of the tombs as *"exceedingly fierce"* (Matthew 8:28). According to Paul, in the last days, "fierce times" are going to come.

Paul gives us the reason for this development. It will not be the result of the rapid advance of technology, scientific discoveries, or the threat of weapons of mass destruction. It will result from the corruption of human nature. Paul writes, *"Men will be…,"* and then he lists eighteen moral and ethical defects that will characterize humanity near the close of this age. If we look at the world today, basically, all of these defects are conspicuous.

One truth about corruption that I learned some years ago through studying Scripture is that corruption is irreversible. Let me offer a simple example. You have a beautiful, ripe peach that is ready to eat. But if you merely leave it on the kitchen counter, it begins to wither and rot. Why? Because the force of corruption is working in it, and nothing can reverse that force. You can put the peach in the refrigerator, and the refrigerator will slow down the process of corruption—but it will not reverse it. I hope you will forgive me for saying this, but I think some churches are like refrigerators. They serve to slow down the process of corruption, but they don't reverse it. God does not tell us to try to slow down corruption—He says that you and I must be born again. We must have a totally new start, a new nature that is free from the corruption of sin.

LOVERS OF SELF

Interestingly, out of the eighteen features Paul lists, the first one is that people will be *"lovers of self,"* and then second, *"lovers of money."* At the end of the list is *"lovers of pleasure."* Can you think of three phrases that better describe the culture in which we live today? Love of self, love of money, and love of pleasure.

The key word is love of *self.* I believe that is the root out of which all the rest will grow. When we begin to love ourselves more than anyone or anything else, society breaks down. It is self-love—in the sense of selfishness or self-absorption—that breaks up marriages and families. A man says to his wife, "If you don't like the way I live, I can find another wife." The wife says the same words to her husband. Parents say, "We want to lead our own lives—we don't want to be tied down by focusing on our children." And they begin to pursue their own selfish desires at the expense of their children.

Similarly, the political realm in most nations today is essentially dominated by self-interest and various pressure groups seeking their own agenda. Very few of them have any real concern for the welfare of their nations. What is the problem? Self-love.

I believe that out of this deep root of self-love comes the breakdown of the family, which leads to the breakdown of society, which leads to anarchy. If I am right in this assessment, from anarchy comes tyranny, despotism, and dictatorship. I believe many national governments will crumble into anarchy, and out of desperation, the people will accept dictatorships in order to restore order and stability. There will be one final dictatorship—the worse one of all—the rule of the antichrist. I believe this is the direction in which the world is headed, and I believe the hour has grown later than most of us are willing to admit.

You might say, "Well, history is full of examples of what you've been talking about." That is true. But I think none of those historical examples occurred on the same scale and with the same worldwide manifestation of what we are seeing today.

ONE UNPARALLELED EVENT

There is one unique feature of this age, however, that has not been present since the first century: the presence of the Jewish people in their own country. Their regathering in the twentieth century led to the creation of the State of Israel. There is no parallel to that milestone in any previous century, and I believe this is *the* decisive indication of how near we are to the close of the age. It has been said that the Jewish people are the minute hand on God's prophetic clock. By my reading of the clock, the minute hand stands at about two minutes to midnight.

The prophet Jeremiah clearly prophesied the regathering of Israel:

"For behold, the days are coming," says the Lord, "that I will bring back from captivity my people Israel and Judah," says the Lord. "And I will cause them to return to the land that I gave to their fathers, and they shall possess it."   (Jeremiah 30:3)

Without question, there is only one land God gave to the forefathers of the Jewish people. That is the land that is called Israel today. The mere restoration of the name of Israel is one of the most significant features of our age.

My first wife, Lydia, and I were living in Jerusalem when the State of Israel was born. Almost to the last moment, the leaders were debating what name to give it. Many were very much in favor of "Judea." But you see, that name would have been contrary to Scripture. Why? Because God had said when the Jewish people returned to their land, they would no longer be divided into the southern kingdom of Judah and the northern kingdom of Israel. There would be one kingdom. At the last moment, the name *Israel* was chosen. God had His hand in that decision.

In connection with this, at the end of Jeremiah 30, the Lord says, "*In the latter days you will consider it*" (verse 24). Several other translations say, "*…you will understand this.*" So the restoration of the Jewish people to their own land is something that indicates we are in the latter days.

THEIR QUESTION, OUR QUESTION

Not long before His suffering and death, Jesus's disciples asked Him this question: "*What will be the sign of Your coming, and of the end of the age?*" (Matthew 24:3). Over two thousand years later, we are asking the same question.

Here is Jesus's reply: "*But of that day and hour no one knows, not even the angels of heaven, but My Father only. But as the days of Noah were, so also will the coming of the Son of Man be*" (Matthew 24:36–37).

We don't know when the Lord will return in glory. But as we have seen in this chapter, one of the indicators will be societal factors like those in the days of Noah and Lot. It is evident that we are living in times that are extraordinarily similar to those very days. In the next chapter, we will continue our discussion about how we are to meet the challenges of living in this unprecedented period of history.

32

UNCHARTED TERRITORY

As believers, we are facing two distinct possibilities in the coming years: the crumbling of present world systems and the simultaneous possibility of a great harvest for God. How are we to prepare?

WHAT TO EXPECT

It seems as if there is nothing really permanent or reliable that you and I can count on at this point in history. I grew up in England between World War I and World War II. There were many problems at that time, including rampant poverty, oppression of the poor by the rich, and numerous political crises. Even with all that, Britain was basically a very secure country. You knew where you belonged. You knew what to expect. You knew you could rely on the police. Essentially, there was not much political corruption. This was also basically true of Europe, the United States, and most of the countries of the West. But all that has totally changed, and it has changed within a very short span of time.

Young people who are high school age and older are stepping out into uncharted territory. There isn't any real human map to advise them on which way to go or what to expect. But I believe the tremendous challenges we face also mean tremendous opportunities! There is counsel in the Bible that will enable us to make a success of our lives.

In the truest sense of the word, I believe God intends every believer to be *successful*. I am not talking about being conspicuously wealthy or even highly educated. But *every child of God*—and that includes you and me— *is born to overcome*. We were born to meet the challenge of living in this unique age and overcoming it. We were born to lead a life that ultimately will leave behind consequences of eternal importance. That is my estimate of what it is to be a child of God, in whatever age of history God has placed us.

THE COUNSEL WE NEED

In order to experience the success God wants for us, we will have to follow the counsel of the Word of God. One of the most important decisions we can make involves where we will receive our counsel from. The first verse of Psalm 1 reads, *"Blessed is the man who walks not in the counsel of the ungodly."* That sets the whole tone for the book of Psalms.

Let me ask you: Where do you get your counsel from? Where do you get your advice? Who directs your thinking? Is it from some form of secular thinking, or some form of higher education?

I was steeped in higher education. Additionally, I had achieved a certain degree of status in the academic world of Britain. I will tell you something about universities—they are very closed places. They are little islands of their own. In many ways, they are cut off from the realities of life. There is also a whole lot of "fashion" that comes and goes in intellectual thinking. When I was studying philosophy in the 1930s, the great philosophy—the "fashion" of that time—was linguistic philosophy. I was a pupil of the great leader of that movement, Ludwig Wittgenstein. Yet, since those prestigious days, the intellectual fashion has changed completely. Today, people are not interested in "linguistic philosophy." There are other fads and fancies. So, believe me, if you rely on human wisdom to guide you, you may end up in a muddled place of chaos and confusion. There is only one reliable source of guidance. What is it? The Bible.

That is why, in my teaching, I concentrate on words of counsel from the Bible. As I prepared this study, I realized that I personally did not have anything new to say—the Bible has already said it all. All I have to do is share what the Bible has already revealed.

The Bible is a timeless book. It applies in any age, in any culture, and to any group of people. I have had the privilege of teaching the Bible to people of many different nationalities, cultures, and languages. It is the only book I know that reaches every human being, wherever they are, and from whatever background they may have.

ALIGN WITH GOD'S PRIORITIES

My first word of counsel is this: align your life with God's priorities. In other words, make God's priorities your own priorities. If you do that, you will have placed yourself in line for the blessings, protection, and provision of God. (See Matthew 6:33.)

How can you know God's priorities? He has stated them very clearly in a passage of the New Testament which is perhaps the most familiar of all—a section we call "the Lord's Prayer." This prayer begins by giving glory to the Father. Then comes a petition—the one that takes precedence over all others:

Your kingdom come. Your will be done on earth as it is in heaven.
(Matthew 6:10)

This is priority number one for God—the coming of His kingdom on earth in the person of His chosen King, Jesus. If you are not lined up with this as your priority, you will find yourself out of harmony with God. You will find yourself in situations where you don't have the answer and you don't know how to respond.

Thus, the first step you need to take is to make up your mind that this is your priority: "What is most important in my life is that the kingdom of God would come on the earth through Jesus Christ." If you can't align yourself with this priority, don't pray the Lord's Prayer, because that will mean you are a hypocrite. The first specific petition of the Lord's Prayer is, *"Your kingdom come."*

How many millions of people pray these words and never realize what they are praying for? They are articulating His priority number one. Everything that is happening in human history is being directed by God to that one conclusion—the coming of His kingdom on earth.

POSITIONED IN GOD'S PURPOSES

Why should we pray for God's kingdom to come? Because the earth has no other hope. If we have to depend on what the politicians can do, may God help us! They have had a lot of time, money, and power to implement their plans, but the world is in a worse mess today than it has ever been.

Isn't it amazing that there are people foolish enough to believe that somehow politicians will get us out of this mess? I don't believe they can. I believe we have an obligation to pray for our political leaders. But I don't expect our salvation to come from them or from any political party. None of them has the answer. Maybe some of them are a little closer to the truth than others, but it is very hard to know with any certainty.

Some years ago, the conservative Christians in the United States were very disappointed when a particularly liberal candidate was elected president. After the election, when Ruth and I arrived back at the office to talk with the members of our staff, they were all sitting around looking very gloomy. I said, "What are you worrying about? This president can't make America any worse than it already is."

If we do not align ourselves with God's priorities, we will not prosper. I saw this precise reality come to pass in the destiny of the British Empire. I was living in what was then Palestine during the closing years of the British mandate in the mid-1940s. Without saying it publicly, the British officials did everything in their power short of open war to prevent the birth of the State of Israel. However, Israel was born—and the British Empire fell apart.

Have you ever considered the connection between those two events? The British Empire had survived two major world wars, maintaining a degree of prosperity and strength. There were only a few times in history when Britain was ever defeated in war. However, taking a stand against God's purpose for Israel terminated the power of the British Empire. The same can take place with any nation which opposes God's plans for the nation of Israel. A nation cannot align itself against God's purposes and still prosper—and neither can you or I.

Our first priority needs to be committing our lives to God and to His kingdom coming on earth through Jesus Christ. In doing so, we will be aligned with His ultimate purposes.

33

AN UNSHAKABLE KINGDOM

In the previous chapter, we saw how important alignment with God's purposes can be for any nation, or any individual, to prosper. In the end, no other kingdom but God's will be left standing. This truth is vividly portrayed for us in Hebrews 12:25–28:

> *See that you do not refuse Him who speaks* [God]. *For if they did not escape who refused Him who spoke on earth, much more shall we not escape if we turn away from Him who speaks from heaven* [God speaking from heaven through His Son Jesus Christ], *whose voice then shook the earth; but now He has promised, saying, "Yet once more I shake not only the earth, but also heaven." Now this, "Yet once more," indicates the removal of those things that are being shaken, as of things that are made, that the things which cannot be shaken may remain. Therefore, since we are receiving a kingdom which cannot be shaken, let us have grace, by which we may serve God acceptably with reverence and godly fear.*

Do you believe that what this passage promises about a shaking is true? I do. I believe this is exactly what is going to happen. What will be God's purpose for permitting a worldwide shaking? It will be to establish and highlight what *cannot* be shaken.

LIFE ON THE ROCK

There is only one kingdom that cannot be shaken. It is not the kingdom of Great Britain, China, Russia, Brazil, the United States, or any other nation on the face of the earth. It is not an earthly kingdom. It is the kingdom of God—it is the kingdom that is founded on Jesus Christ. Jesus Himself said that if you and I build on this foundation, no storm will overthrow what we build. (See Matthew 7:24–25.)

Everything else that can be shaken will be shaken—and most of it is being shaken right now. Ask yourself this question: "What are some of the institutions that can be shaken?" Governments? There is scarcely a government on earth that isn't being shaken at the moment. What about banks? Can banks be shaken? They certainly can. Financial institutions and entire economies are being shaken. What about church denominations? Can they be shaken? Yes. Many denominations are being shaken to their very core. Can families be shaken? Yes, they can—and they are being severely shaken in our modern times. Only the families that are built on the Rock, Jesus Christ, will be able to survive.

WHO WILL STAND?

The Lord is sorting everything into one of two categories: what can be shaken and what cannot be shaken. You and I need to know where we stand. Are we truly in the kingdom that cannot be shaken? If not, we are going to collapse. There will be a shaking of everything the world has trusted in, but the kingdom of God will pass through the shaking unmoved. Believe me, we will not be exempt from the shaking. But the result will be different in our lives. We will stand when everything else collapses all around us.

In Haggai 2:7, God declares, *"I will shake all nations."* This shaking includes every nation on the face of the earth—rich or poor, democratic or despotic, civilized or uncivilized. God is going to shake all nations, and we must be prepared. In the coming time of shaking, there will be only one kind of person who cannot be shaken. Such a person is described in 1 John 2:

Do not love the world or the things in the world.　　　　　　(verse 15)

In the original Greek, the phrase translated *"the world"* means the social system. The present world system is "the world." John says, "Don't love the present world system." Let me say to young people, especially: do not fall in love with the world!

After this admonition, John makes a very serious statement:

If anyone loves the world, the love of the Father is not in him.
(1 John 2:15)

In other words, we cannot have it both ways. We cannot love the world and love God at the same time. In chapter 9 of *The Coming Revival*, we saw that God's love is a jealous love. He will not tolerate our loyalty to the world. You and I have to make up our minds as to where we will place our affections and our priorities.

For all that is in the world—the lust of the flesh, the lust of the eyes, and the pride of life—is not of the Father but is of the world. And the world is passing away, and the lust of it; but he who does the will of God abides forever. (1 John 2:16–17)

The lusts described in verse 17 are not only based upon a love for the world, but they are also passing away. Bear in mind that they are on their way out—and we will be, as well, if we cling to them. The world is passing away, but the person who does the will of God *"abides forever."*

Who is the only unshakable person on earth today? The one who is totally committed to the will of God. If you want to have a successful future in today's world, my counsel to you is to commit yourself without reservation to the will of God for your life. You will abide forever. You will be unshakable. You will be as unshakable as the will of God itself—because you will be identified with God's will.

SEEK FIRST THE KINGDOM

Clearly, this process of purifying ourselves and dedicating ourselves totally to God's will and kingdom must be our priority. In today's success-oriented culture, the idea of prioritizing what is important to you is

222 The Coming Revival

a very popular theme. But the truth is, maintaining right priorities is paramount in the Christian life. Your priorities will decide the direction and outcome of your life. Whatever has top priority in your life is what you will find time for.

Some people say, "I can't find any time to read the Bible." However, they find time to eat! Whatever you give your time to indicates your priorities. I am not saying it is wrong to eat, but I am saying that the Bible is actually more important than food. Here is God's counsel on our priorities, given to us by Jesus:

> But seek first the kingdom of God and His righteousness, and all these
> things shall be added to you.   (Matthew 6:33)

"All these things" means everything you need for daily life: food, clothing, housing, transportation—whatever it may be. God says if you will seek His kingdom first, He will take care of every other need.

Throughout my life as a Christian, I have had moments of weakness and temptation. But I have tried to live according to this principle as faithfully as I could. I want to declare that God has *always* been faithful to me. He has provided everything I needed. I am not propounding a theory here. It is a reality based on Scripture that has been substantiated over and over in my own experience. I know many other friends who could give the same testimony. They also have sought the kingdom of God first and found Him faithful. They would also say He has taken care of every need in their lives.

To summarize, this is my counsel: Get your priorities right. Line up with the will of God from this moment forward. Make it a new passion in your life to align yourself fully with the Lord. Place yourself squarely on the Rock. Then, you can stand firm when all else is being shaken.

34

MARKS OF PREPARATION

God is going to establish His kingdom on earth. But He is also looking for a people who will share in His kingdom. There is a beautiful passage of Scripture that I have regularly proclaimed. It expresses this principle of the people God seeks much more clearly than I ever could:

> *The grace of God that brings salvation has appeared to all men, teaching us that, denying ungodliness and worldly lusts, we should live soberly, righteously, and godly in the present age, looking for the blessed hope and glorious appearing of our great God and Savior Jesus Christ, who gave Himself for us, that He might redeem us from every lawless deed and purify for Himself His own special people, zealous for good works.* (Titus 2:11–14)

A SPECIAL PEOPLE

God's first priority is the coming of His kingdom on earth in the person of His chosen King—Jesus. His second priority is *"His own special people."* This passage declares that Jesus will purify His people. But there is another aspect to this purification that is revealed in 1 John 3:1–3:

> *Behold what manner of love the Father has bestowed on us, that we should be called children of God! Therefore the world does not know*

223

us, because it did not know Him. Beloved, now we are children of God;
and it has not yet been revealed what we shall be, but we know that
when He is revealed, we shall be like Him, for we shall see Him as He
is. And everyone who has this hope in Him purifies himself, just as He
is pure.

Please notice John's words: *"Everyone who has this hope in Him **purifies**
himself, just as He is pure."* We can say as much as we want about how we
are eagerly waiting for the coming of the Lord. But if we are not purifying
ourselves in preparation for this great event, we are only deceiving ourselves. The mark of all who are truly waiting for the coming of the Lord is
that they are purifying themselves, *"just as He is pure."* God has only one
standard of purity—and it is Jesus.

THE BEAUTY OF HOLINESS

I frequently say to young people, especially young women, "It is very
natural to want to look pretty and to have a pleasing appearance. There is
nothing wrong or sinful about that. However, it is *external*. There is a different kind of beauty that is internal. When your external attractiveness
begins to fade, this beauty will never fade—it is the purity and holiness of
God."

The holiness of God is true spiritual beauty. We may do all we can to
be pretty or handsome. But we need to bear in mind that real beauty is
found within us. It shines out of the eyes of the people who have it. They
look different. They act different. They speak different. They don't have to
be religious. They just have to be pure.

There is a deep hunger for purity in the hearts of multitudes of people
in the world today. You will find that hunger in all sorts of places—among
prostitutes, among prisoners, among alcoholics, among hard-boiled busi-
nessmen. Somewhere deep down there is a longing for purity. We can tell
people how to find their way to that purity. What is that way? To give your
life unreservedly to Jesus Christ. He will purify you. In giving yourself to
Him, you will find the way to the purity for which you long.

SEVEN MARKS OF PREPARATION

As we draw closer to the end of this study, let's look at seven marks of spiritual preparation given to us by the apostle Peter in 2 Peter 3:11–14. In this passage, which deals with the coming of the Lord and the day of the Lord, Peter admonishes those who are genuinely preparing themselves for that day:

> *Therefore, since all these things* [the entire material universe] *will be dissolved, what manner of persons ought you to be in holy conduct and godliness, looking for and hastening the coming of the day of God, because of which the heavens will be dissolved, being on fire, and the elements will melt with fervent heat? Nevertheless we, according to His promise, look for new heavens and a new earth in which righteousness dwells. Therefore, beloved, looking forward to these things, be diligent to be found by Him in peace, without spot and blameless.*
>
> (2 Peter 3:11–14)

HOLY CONDUCT

What sort of people ought we to be? If you analyze the above passage, there are seven requirements for a Christian who is truly looking forward to the coming of the Lord. In 2 Peter 3:11, we see that the first two requirements are *"holy conduct,"* or holy living, and *"godliness."* My definition of godliness is having a temperament controlled by the Holy Spirit. A godly person's reactions proceed from the Spirit.

What really tells the world around us what we are like is not our actions—it is our *reactions*. Our actions can be premeditated. But our reactions reveal what kind of person we really are because they are spontaneous. Godliness reacts in the way the Holy Spirit would react. When a godly person walks into a room, the presence of God walks in with them.

AWAITING CHRIST'S RETURN

In 2 Peter 3:12, we find two more requirements: *"looking for...the coming of the day of God"* and *"hastening"* that day. The writer of Hebrews echoes this thought:

> *And as it is appointed for men to die once, but after this the judgment, so Christ was offered once to bear the sins of many. To those who eagerly wait for Him He will appear a second time, apart from sin, for salvation.* (Hebrews 9:27–28)

To whom will Jesus appear? To those who eagerly wait for Him. Let me ask you: are you eagerly waiting for the appearing of the Lord? If not, the Lord may let you go through some unpleasant experiences to wean you from the love of this world. Only then will you come to the conclusion, in a very practical way, that there is nothing really to look forward to but the coming of the Lord.

Please note that this verse does not say Jesus is coming for "church members." He is coming for believers who are eagerly awaiting His appearance.

Peter says we must be looking for and hastening the coming of the day of God. That is a powerful thought—that we can hasten the coming of the day of God. We don't need to sit passively and just wait for it to happen. We can actually hasten its coming! Do you remember this very obvious way to hasten the coming of the Lord?

> *And this gospel of the kingdom will be preached in all the world as a witness to all the nations, and then the end will come.* (Matthew 24:14)

The end will not come until the gospel of Jesus Christ has been preached in all the world to all the nations. We have a vital part to play in this endeavor. I believe every true Christian has a responsibility to participate in the preaching of the gospel. We cannot personally go to all the nations. But we can be involved in prayer, in giving, and in supporting individuals and organizations who are actively carrying out this work.

Can we assume, then, that anyone who is not in some way involved in the preaching of the gospel of the kingdom to all nations is delaying the coming of the Lord? That is a fearful responsibility. Think of all the unbearable agony and suffering in the world today. Why is this happening? Because the kingdom of God has not yet been established. And the longer we have to wait, the greater will be the toll of human suffering. We have a responsibility to hasten the coming of the day of the Lord. If we do not do this, we will ultimately be held accountable for the suffering that results from our laziness.

If we search the Bible from beginning to end, there is never a good word about laziness. In most of our churches, we will not accept drunkenness, but the Bible is much kinder about drunkenness than it is about laziness. Laziness is wickedness. Let us never allow laziness to delay the coming of the kingdom of God.

LIVING IN PEACE

In 2 Peter 3:14, we find three more requirements:

Therefore, beloved, looking forward to these things, be diligent to be found by Him in peace, without spot and blameless.

The final requirements are *"in peace, without spot and blameless." "In peace,"* the fifth requirement, means you have no ruptured relationships that you need to mend in your family, in your church, or even with your unsaved neighbors. To the best of your ability, are you living in peace with those around you? Paul admonishes us to keep peace with all men as far as it depends on us. (See Romans 12:18.) Of course, there are some situations that are out of our control. But God says that insofar as possible, let there be no broken relationships, unresolved resentments, or bitterness.

Ruth and I were once in a very difficult situation with a neighbor who was trying to manipulate us. She wanted us to do something we felt we had no obligation to do, and she became very difficult to deal with—strident, vocal, and antagonistic. Finally, I said to Ruth, "I am not going to give way to manipulation. This is witchcraft." So we prayed a fervent prayer of agreement, driving witchcraft out of that situation. Then, something miraculous happened. A little while later, this neighbor told Ruth, "I want to tell you that I've had asthma. And when I have asthma, I get very nervous and I shout and scream at people. Forgive me, I'm sorry." She ended up becoming our friend. I saw God's wisdom in that process. He would not let us move out of that house until our relationship was right with our neighbors. God cares about our living in peace, and He cares about us *and* our neighbors.

How is it between you and your neighbors? The second most important commandment is, *"Love your neighbor as yourself."* (See, for example, Matthew 22:39.) This really means your actual neighbor—it is not just a figure of speech.

How are you getting on with the people you live closest to? How are you getting on with the people you work next to on the job? If you are preparing for the Lord's coming, you must try to mend your relationships if you are not at peace with those with whom you live and work.

WITHOUT SPOT

The sixth requirement is to be *"without spot."* What does this mean? First Peter 1:19 says, *"…the precious blood of Christ, as of a lamb without blemish or without spot."* I understand this to mean Jesus was without personal original sin, and He also never committed any sin. Either of those would have been a *"spot."*

I believe any sin you or I have committed and have not repented of and confessed is a "spot" on our lives. The Word of God says we have to be without spot, so we must keep short accounts with the Lord. Never go to sleep with unconfessed sin in your life. Who knows if you will wake up? It might be your last night on earth.

BLAMELESS

The seventh requirement is that we must be *"blameless."* I understand this to mean we have not neglected any legitimate duty. Whatever our duty is, we have done it.

James writes, *"To him who knows to do good and does not do it, to him it is sin"* (James 4:17). If you know of any good actions that you should and can take, but you do not do them, that is sin, something for which you can be "blamed."

Let's review the seven requirements from 2 Peter 3:11–14:

1. Holy conduct
2. Godliness

3. Looking for the coming of the Lord

4. Hastening the coming of the Lord

5. Being in peace

6. Being without spot

7. Being blameless

This teaching from the apostle Peter enables us to know what sort of person we ought to be as the coming day of the Lord draws near. It is a helpful list for us as we seek to purify ourselves in these perilous times.

35

THE TIME IS SHORT

Now we come to one closing passage that is for people of all ages. But it is especially for young people. It deals partly with the subject of marriage.

It is remarkable that Paul wrote these words about twenty centuries ago, and yet they are so true today:

> But this I say, brethren, the time is short [If it was short then, how much shorter is it now?], so that from now on even those who have wives should be as though they have none, those who weep as though they did not weep, those who rejoice as though who did not rejoice, those who buy as though they did not possess, and those who use this world as not misusing it. For the form [or fashion] of this world is passing away. (1 Corinthians 7:29–31)

What message is this passage bringing to those who are not married? "Don't be in a hurry to get married." I have seen many young men and women get married. Basically, I have observed that the ones who were over-eager to get married tended to make a mess of their marriages. On the other hand, the ones who waited patiently for God's appointment have had successful marriages. *Single people should not be in a hurry to get married.* If you move too fast, it may be because you have made marriage an idol. When someone makes marriage their idol, it can take the place of Jesus in their lives.

I am not saying it is wrong to get married. It would be ridiculous for me to say that because I have been married twice! And I am satisfied. But I cannot overemphasize the importance of *waiting* for God's appointment for marriage.

KEEPING AN OPEN HAND

Did you catch the essence of what Paul is saying in the above passage? He is telling us not to hold on to anything temporal as if it were permanent. We are to live with a sense of impermanence in regard to anything material and every human relationship. He then goes on to say,

> *But I want you to be without care* [without anxiety or worry]. *He who is unmarried cares for the things of the Lord—how he may please the Lord. But he who is married cares about the things of the world—how he may please his wife.* (1 Corinthians 7:32–33)

Please don't misunderstand Paul's intent. He is not speaking against marriage. He has a lot of good words to say about marriage. What is he saying? Don't give marriage a place of wrong importance in your thinking. Don't make it your ambition. Don't go out with an agenda to find a wife or a husband.

Both times when I married, God brought the woman of His choice to me. *I never went out looking.* If you read the true romantic stories of the Bible, this is nearly always the case—God brought the bride to the bridegroom. He brought Rebekah to Isaac. He brought Ruth to Boaz. If we trust God, He will choose much better for us than we can choose for ourselves. Do you believe that? My advice to you is this: don't put marriage before the Lord. Instead, wait. Wait for the Lord to work.

In fact, don't put *anything* before the Lord. That is what Paul is saying. Don't hold on to *anything* in this world as if it were permanent, because it is not. If you do hold on to something and it is taken from you, you will suffer emotionally—and maybe spiritually too.

A WITNESS TO THE NATIONS

We have now come to the end of our study, and I want to offer a final practical application. As a basis for this practical advice, let's look again at Matthew 24:14:

And this gospel of the kingdom will be preached in all the world as a witness to all the nations, and then the end will come.

As I have noted, I believe this proclamation places an obligation on every sincere Christian to be totally committed—in one way or another—to the preaching of the gospel of the kingdom in all the world. There are many different ways you can be committed to this. However, I want to speak primarily to young people now—you who have the opportunity to give your life to this task. I am not necessarily asking you to be a missionary or an evangelist, because the kingdom of God needs secretaries, administrators, cooks, and pilots as well—all kinds of people with all kinds of vocations. Each vocation is as important as the other.

However, if you sense that God is speaking to you, I want to encourage you to respond to Him with all your heart. You may not know right now what your life is supposed to be. You may not really know what you are living for. You might recognize that you are not really committed to something that demands your total loyalty.

In view of all those factors, I want to ask you this question: Would you put your life in the Lord's hands right now? Would you say to Him, "Here I am, Lord, wholly available to You?"

There was a song that was sung regularly in the Anglican church where Ruth and I attended services in Jerusalem. The first words of the chorus were, "Here I am, wholly available." I could always say those words with a clear conscience: "Here I am, Lord, wholly available. Whatever You ask, by Your grace, I'll do it." And I am satisfied. I am fulfilled. I have lived my life that way, and I can tell you—it works.

234 The Coming Revival

TOTAL DEVOTION

If you have never really made that commitment, would you consider making it now? Are you ready to say these words to the Lord? "Here I am. Use me in whatever way You wish—and send me wherever You choose."

There are so many areas of need! A nurse is needed somewhere. A secretary is needed somewhere. A gardener is needed somewhere. Ruth and I received a letter from a man who said he is a gardener, and he wants to garden for the Lord. He is making himself available to anybody who needs a gardener for God's kingdom.

So, whoever you are and whatever you are doing, make yourself available to Him. You can have the fulfillment of living according to Matthew 6:33: "*Seek first the kingdom of God and His righteousness, and all these things shall be added to you.*"

I hope you will make that decision. If you wish to make this commitment, I want you to say, right where you are at this moment, "Here I am, wholly available."

This is a very, very serious moment in your life. There will probably never be a more significant moment than this one. I hope I have made it difficult enough. I hope I haven't given you a wrong impression that it is going to be easy from here on. It is not. You will experience opposition—the devil is going to fight you from this moment onward, attempting to attack your commitment to the Lord. You are going to be a target for Satan's assaults as you have never been before.

But, if you are ready, I want you to say this very simple prayer to the Lord Jesus. Would you say these words?

Lord Jesus Christ, thank You for dying for me on the cross so that I might be saved from hell and have eternal life. Because of what You have done for me, I give myself back to You without reservation, unconditionally. Here I am, wholly available. Take me, Lord, and make me what You want me to be, for Your glory. In Jesus's name. Amen.

Now, to seal the commitment you have just made, why not recite the lyrics to "Here I Am, Wholly Available" out loud?

"HERE I AM, WHOLLY AVAILABLE"

Here I am, wholly available.
As for me, I will serve the Lord.

The fields are white unto the harvest,
But O, the laborers are so few.
So Lord, I give myself to help the reaping
To gather precious souls unto You.

Here I am, wholly available.
As for me, I will serve the Lord.

The time is right in the nations
For works of power and authority.
God's looking for a people who are willing
To be counted in His glorious victory.

Here I am, wholly available.
As for me, I will serve the Lord.

As salt, are we ready to savor,
In darkness, are we ready to be light?
God's seeking out a very special people
To manifest His truth and His might.

Here I am, wholly available.
As for me, I will serve the Lord.

ABOUT THE AUTHOR

Derek Prince (1915–2003) was born in India of British parents. He was educated as a scholar of Greek and Latin at Eton College and King's College, Cambridge, in England. Upon graduation, he held a fellowship (equivalent to a professorship) in Ancient and Modern Philosophy at King's College. Prince also studied Hebrew, Aramaic, and modern languages at Cambridge and the Hebrew University in Jerusalem. As a student, he was a philosopher and a self-proclaimed agnostic.

While serving in the British Medical Corps during World War II, Prince began to study the Bible as a philosophical work. Converted through a powerful encounter with Jesus Christ, he was baptized in the Holy Spirit a few days later. Out of this encounter, he formed two conclusions: first, that Jesus Christ is alive; second, that the Bible is a true, relevant, up-to-date book. These conclusions altered the whole course of his life, which he then devoted to studying and teaching the Bible as the Word of God.

Discharged from the army in Jerusalem in 1945, he married Lydia Christensen, founder of a children's home there. Upon their marriage, he immediately became father to Lydia's eight adopted daughters—six Jewish, one Palestinian Arab, and one English. Together, the family saw the rebirth of the state of Israel in 1948. In the late 1950s, they adopted another daughter while Prince was serving as principal of a teachers' training college in Kenya.

In 1963, the Princes immigrated to the United States and pastored a church in Seattle. In 1973, Prince became one of the founders of Intercessors for America. His book Shaping History through Prayer and Fasting has awakened Christians around the world to their responsibility to pray for their governments. Many consider underground translations of the book as instrumental in the fall of communist regimes in the USSR, East Germany, and Czechoslovakia.

Lydia Prince died in 1975, and Prince married Ruth Baker (a single mother to three adopted children) in 1978. He met his second wife, like his first wife, while she was serving the Lord in Jerusalem. Ruth died in December 1998 in Jerusalem, where they had lived since 1981.

Until a few years before his own death in 2003 at the age of eighty-eight, Prince persisted in the ministry God had called him to as he traveled the world, imparting God's revealed truth, praying for the sick and afflicted, and sharing his prophetic insights into world events in the light of Scripture. Internationally recognized as a Bible scholar and spiritual patriarch, Derek Prince established a teaching ministry that spanned six continents and more than sixty years. He is the author of more than eighty books, six hundred audio teachings, and one hundred video teachings, many of which have been translated and published in more than one hundred languages. He pioneered teaching on such groundbreaking themes as generational curses, the biblical significance of Israel, and demonology.

Prince's radio program, which began in 1979, has been translated into more than a dozen languages and continues to touch lives. Derek Prince's main gift of explaining the Bible and its teachings in a clear and simple way has helped build a foundation of faith in millions of lives. His nondenominational, nonsectarian approach has made his teaching equally relevant and helpful to people from all racial and religious backgrounds, and his messages are estimated to have reached more than half the globe.

In 2002, he said, "It is my desire—and I believe the Lord's desire—that this ministry continue the work, which God began through me over sixty years ago, until Jesus returns."

Derek Prince Ministries continues to reach out to believers in over 140 countries with Derek's teaching, fulfilling the mandate to keep on "until Jesus returns." This is accomplished through the outreaches of more than forty-five Derek Prince offices around the world, including primary work in Australia, Canada, China, France, Germany, the Netherlands, New Zealand, Norway, Russia, South Africa, Switzerland, the United Kingdom, and the United States. For current information about these and other worldwide locations, visit www.derekprince.org.

Welcome to Our House!

We Have a Special Gift for You

It is our privilege and pleasure to share in your love of Christian books. We are committed to bringing you authors and books that feed, challenge, and enrich your faith.

To show our appreciation, we invite you to sign up to receive a specially selected **Reader Appreciation Gift**, with our compliments. Just go to the Web address at the bottom of this page.

God bless you as you seek a deeper walk with Him!

WE HAVE A GIFT FOR YOU. VISIT:

whpub.me/nonfictionthx

WHITAKER
HOUSE